10 JUDGEMENTS
THAT CHANGED INDIA

10 JUDGEMENTS
THAT CHANGED INDIA

ZIA MODY

FOREWORD BY SOLI J. SORABJEE

Sdé
Shobhaa Dé
BOOKS

SHOBHAA DÉ BOOKS

Published by the Penguin Group

Penguin Books India Pvt. Ltd, 7th Floor, Infinity Tower C, DLF Cyber City, Gurgaon 122 002, Haryana, India

Penguin Group (USA) Inc., 375 Hudson Street, New York, New York 10014, USA

Penguin Group (Canada), 90 Eglinton Avenue East, Suite 700, Toronto, Ontario, M4P 2Y3, Canada

Penguin Books Ltd, 80 Strand, London WC2R 0RL, England

Penguin Ireland, 25 St Stephen's Green, Dublin 2, Ireland (a division of Penguin Books Ltd)

Penguin Group (Australia), 707 Collins Street, Melbourne, Victoria 3008, Australia

Penguin Group (NZ), 67 Apollo Drive, Rosedale, Auckland 0632, New Zealand

Penguin Group (South Africa) (Pty) Ltd, Block D, Rosebank Office Park, 181 Jan Smuts Avenue, Parktown North, Johannesburg 2193, South Africa

Penguin Books Ltd, Registered Offices: 80 Strand, London WC2R 0RL, England

First published in Shobhaa Dé books by Penguin books India 2013

ISBN 9780670086627

Typeset in adobe Garamond by R. ajith kumar, New Delhi
Printed at Replika Press Pvt. Ltd, India

A PENGUIN RANDOM HOUSE COMPANY

To my father, Soli Sorabjee,
who is the inspiration behind this book.

To my mother, Zena, for all her encouragement, always.

To Jaydev, my husband, for his unending support and pride.

To my three princesses, Anjali, Aarti and Aditi,
whose unadulterated love keeps me moving on.

ACKNOWLEDGEMENTS

WRITING THIS BOOK would not have been possible without the involvement of a few people. Shobhaa Dé was the pioneer behind the idea of writing a book of this nature which seeks to bridge the gap between life and the law. Mudita Chauhan-Mubayi, Madhavi Purohit, Shahnaz Siganporia and the editorial team of Penguin Books India have all regularly provided constructive suggestions to make this book engaging for a wider spectrum of readers. Chintan Chandrachud's exhaustive legal research and keen drafting skills have taken the book from conception to reality—to him I owe an immeasurable thank you. Jeet Shroff and Rishika Harish have also assiduously assisted in the publication of this book for which I am truly grateful.

CONTENTS

FOREWORD

THE JUDICIARY, AT one time, was considered and projected to be the weakest branch of the state because it possessed neither power of the purse nor power of the sword. That myth has been demolished and the best evidence of it is the set of ten judgements analysed and discussed in this book. Many of the judgements that have been discussed were recognized, even at the time of their pronouncement, as path-breaking and having a profound impact on our nation. To find them being discussed several years later is indeed a testament to their continuing and pervasive relevance.

The Constitution, enacted in 1950, has been the cornerstone of India's democracy. After its enactment it has undergone several amendments. The Supreme Court is the ultimate interpreter of the Constitution and, by its creative and innovative interpretation, has been the protector of our constitutional rights and fundamental freedoms. The Supreme Court judgement in *Kesavananda Bharati v. State of Kerala* (AIR 1973 SC 1461) is unique in its impact. It evolved the doctrine of the 'basic structure' of the Constitution and ruled that even a constitutional amendment could be invalidated if it impaired the essential features—the basic structure—of the Constitution.

The book highlights instances of the manner in which the Supreme Court has performed its role and captures some of the more significant moments in its long and sometimes troubled history.

The judgements described in this book continue to have a real and resounding impact on society as a whole. These decisions are to be appreciated not only as precedents, but also as having laid down the law on issues of paramount importance—law that is binding on all courts and authorities in the country. In a maturing republic such as ours, the common man must be made aware of and given an understanding of the workings of the law and the judicial process, which very often is seen as the exclusive domain of the legal profession. This book is a step in that direction. Rather than focusing just on the judgements of the court, the author has presented them in context, describing the surrounding cultural and social circumstances and the subsequent reactions of the public and the state to each case, coupled with a commendable legal analysis in language that is not legalese, but reader-friendly.

Zia Mody has made a captivating analysis which, I am sure, will be useful not just for members of the legal profession, but also for parliamentarians, law teachers, students and members of the public who are keen to know about our powerful Supreme Court and the impact of its judgements.

Soli J. Sorabjee
Former Attorney-General of India

PROLOGUE

TO A LARGE and obvious extent, the title of this book shapes the prologue and the contents that follow. I believe that if there is one thing that most Indians still remain deeply proud of and have abiding faith in, it is their judiciary. One of the subliminal expectations of the common man is that justice will be delivered by the highest court of the land: the Supreme Court of India. To the intelligentsia, this is the forum in which both political and executive battles will be calibrated and decided. Many of us, especially practising professionals, take much pride in seeing how the Constitution of India has been infused with life, time after time, by a deft, adept, practical and inspired judiciary.

We take for granted, as a democracy, what many citizens in other countries over the world yearn for: the freedom of speech, access to justice, the right to vote and the right to practise one's religion. In this context, every young student of the law clearly comes to recognize both the independence and the importance of the Indian judiciary in our democratic polity.

Selecting ten judgements—those that can be termed 'landmark' cases—involved difficult decisions. The difficulty lay in deciding which judgements not to select simply because—as is evident when one starts looking at the subject—the seminal

cases and landmark jurisprudence laid down by the highest
court of the land have affected the basic liberties of millions
of citizens throughout India. Many a time we tried to bring in
other seminal judgements as part of the selection. For instance,
A.D.M. Jabalpur v. Shivkant Shukla (AIR 1976 SC 1207) has
been discussed in the chapter on *Maneka Gandhi v. Union of
India* (AIR 1978 SC 597) (*Maneka Gandhi*) (Chapter Two);
S.P. Gupta v. President of India (AIR 1982 SC 149) has been
discussed in the chapter analysing *Supreme Court Advocates-on-
Record Association v. Union of India* (AIR 1994 SC 268) (Chapter
Eight); and *Minerva Mills v. Union of India* (AIR 1980 SC 1789)
along with *I.R. Coelho v. State of Tamil Nadu* (AIR 2007 SC 861)
have both been analysed in the chapter discussing *Kesavananda
Bharati v. State of Kerala* (AIR 1973 SC 1461) (Chapter One).

As can be expected, to qualify as landmark decisions, most of
these seminal judgements needed to have a distinct constitutional
angle. It is interesting to see that from 1947 to 2011, in a short
span of sixty-four years, our Constitution has been amended
fairly extensively and interpreted fairly expansively. It is probably
somewhat removed from what our founding fathers would have
anticipated, but, by and large, something they would have been
proud of, with the Supreme Court preserving its 'basic structure'.

Each of the ten judgements decided by the Supreme Court
demonstrates the central role that the court plays in democratic
governance in India. Some of these judgements have arisen as
a result of both the pre- and post-Emergency Indira Gandhi
regime. During this period, the court was in the throes of a
constitutional conflict, torn between deciding on principles
and sometimes, unfortunately, bowing to political exigencies.
However, the guiding light that one hopes will continue is the

ultimate thread of jurisprudence squarely in favour of a strong democracy armed with the unshakeable stamp, the freedom of speech, and the right to life with the other attendant basic constitutional safeguards.

The Emergency probably taught the Supreme Court of India many hard lessons, including, hopefully, some lessons it will never repeat. It also laid bare to the intelligentsia and the common man the fact that respite came from the gates of the courts.

Women dominate as the central figures in four of the ten selected judgements—seen in the cases of *Maneka Gandhi*, *Mohammed Ahmed Khan v. Shah Bano Begum* (AIR 1985 SC 945), *Vishaka v. State of Rajasthan* (AIR 1997 SC 3011) and *Aruna Ramachandra Shanbaug v. Union of India* ((2011) 1 SCALE 673). It not only reflects the tragedy of the Indian woman, but also the emergence of jurisprudence which seeks to set it right. Unfortunately, what remains is the practical reality of a long road yet to be travelled to unwind institutional and cultural discrimination against women.

Many of these cases have had an international impact and have been cited in different countries around the world, particularly in South Asia. The case of *Olga Tellis v. Bombay Municipal Corporation* (AIR 1986 SC 180), dealing with the rights of pavement dwellers, has arguably had a greater impact abroad than in India. As we are prone to do, many of the judgements run into hundreds of pages—but one would rather have prolixity (which leads to somewhat prolific and sometimes over-elaborate prose) than compromise on the quality of justice.

Current events in India—unfolding with Team Anna Hazare capturing the imagination of millions of people and the introduction of the Lokpal Bill (which seeks to constitute an independent anti-corruption ombudsman to curb widespread corruption in India) into Parliament—show how ingrained the DNA of democracy in the minds and hearts of Indian people is, especially of those comprising middle-class India. One would not be wrong in thinking that the Supreme Court's role is likely to be even more urgent, imperative, important and defining in the years to come.

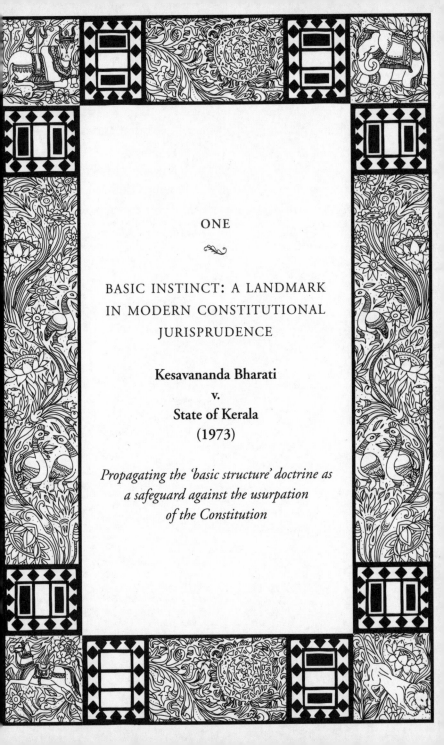

ONE

BASIC INSTINCT: A LANDMARK IN MODERN CONSTITUTIONAL JURISPRUDENCE

Kesavananda Bharati
v.
State of Kerala
(1973)

Propagating the 'basic structure' doctrine as a safeguard against the usurpation of the Constitution

INDIA HAS OFTEN been faced with situations where its paramount democratic institutions have clashed.[1] One such run-in was the struggle for power between the judiciary and the legislature which reached its boiling point in the mid-1970s. In the backdrop of a struggle for constitutional supremacy, the Supreme Court delivered what is arguably the most monumental decision in its history on 24 April 1973. *Kesavananda Bharati v. State of Kerala*[2] (*Kesavananda*) is a case 'unique in the history of international constitutional law'[3] for several reasons: the anxious political circumstances[4] in which it was delivered,[5] the shift in the balance of democratic power it caused, the unprecedented number of separate opinions delivered by the court as well as the sheer length of the judgement itself.

---

1   Milan Dalal, 'India's New Constitutionalism: Two Cases That Have Reshaped Indian Law', *Boston College International and Comparative Law Review*, vol. 31 (2008): p. 257.

2   AIR 1973 SC 1461.

3   V.R. Jayadevan, 'Interpretation of the Amending Clause: The Brawl Between the Spirit of Natural Law and the Ghost of Analytical Positivism—A Comparative Overview of the American and Indian Experiences', *Hamline Law Review*, vol. 33 (2010): p. 243.

4   This included attempts by the Indira Gandhi-led Congress government to pass radical constitutional amendments and place intense political pressure on the Indian judiciary.

5   In the words of Justice Y.V. Chandrachud, the case was fraught with 'unusual happenings' (*see* Granville Austin, *Working a Democratic Constitution: The Indian Experience* (New Delhi: Oxford University Press, 1999), p. 259).

For *Kesavananda*, the Supreme Court sat in judgement for the longest amount of time since its inception[6]—almost five months—to determine issues pivotal to the interaction between and powers of the three conventional branches of government. The judgement, which spans nearly 800 pages and is about 420,000[7] words long, has been named the 'longest appellate decision'[8] of the last century. Apart from its exceptional length, *Kesavananda* was significant in that the Supreme Court ascribed to itself the function of preserving the integrity of the Indian Constitution. The 'basic structure' doctrine formulated by the court represented the pinnacle of judicial creativity[9] and set a benchmark for other constitutional courts around the world, particularly in South Asia.[10]

An analysis of *Kesavananda* is incomplete without a brief discussion of the cases which led up to the Supreme Court's judgement in 1973.

A Conservative Supreme Court: *Shankari Prasad* and *Sajjan Singh*

The struggle for the custody of the Constitution arose from questions concerning the right to property, which (until 1978)

---

6 Gobind Das, 'The Supreme Court: An Overview' in *Supreme But Not Infallible: Essays in Honour of the Supreme Court of India*, eds B.N. Kirpal et al. (New Delhi: Oxford University Press, 2000), pp. 21–22.

7 Vivek Krishnamurthy, 'Colonial Cousins: Explaining India and Canada's Unwritten Constitutional Principles', *The Yale Journal of International Law*, vol. 34 (2009): p. 207.

8 Ibid.

9 Raju Ramachandran, 'The Supreme Court and the Basic Structure Doctrine' in *Supreme But Not Infallible: Essays in Honour of the Supreme Court of India*, eds B.N. Kirpal et al. (New Delhi: Oxford University Press, 2000), p. 108.

10 Whether or not they agreed with the decision in *Kesavananda*, courts in the countries neighbouring India were forced to take notice of the judgement.

was a fundamental right under Article 31. Soon after the Constitution entered into force, agrarian land reform legislation was enacted in Bihar, Uttar Pradesh and Madhya Pradesh. Zamindars[11] thus deprived of a significant portion of their landholdings filed petitions in different high courts alleging that their fundamental right had been infringed. When the Bihar Land Reforms Act, 1950 was invalidated by the Patna High Court in 1951,[12] the Constituent Assembly (functioning then as the provisional Parliament[13]) passed the Constitution (First Amendment) Act, 1951. This amendment inserted two provisions[14] in the Constitution to insulate land reform legislation from judicial scrutiny. One of these provisions, Article 31B, created the Ninth Schedule to the Constitution (which became the subject of sustained judicial examination in several cases discussed later). Any laws inserted (through constitutional amendments) into the Ninth Schedule could not be challenged for being inconsistent with fundamental rights.

Zamindars then challenged the amendment itself in *Shankari Prasad v. Union of India* (*Shankari Prasad*).[15] One of the several grounds of challenge was that the expression 'law' under Article 13(2), which prohibits the Parliament from making any laws that abridge or take away fundamental rights, included not only ordinary laws, but also amendments. If the court accepted this contention it would have implied that Part III of the

---

11 Historically, an Indian landowner; especially one who leases land to tenant farmers.

12 *Kameshwar Singh v. State of Bihar* (AIR 1951 Pat 91) (Patna High Court).

13 Article 379 of the Constitution provided that until both houses of Parliament were duly constituted, the Constituent Assembly was to exercise the powers conferred on the Parliament by the Constitution.

14 Articles 31A and 31B of the Constitution.

15 [1952] 1 SCR 89.

Constitution (which deals with fundamental rights) could never be amended by the Parliament so as to take away or abridge fundamental rights. However, a five-judge bench of the Supreme Court unanimously rejected this argument, asserting that the constitutional scheme provided for a clear demarcation between 'ordinary law, which is made in exercise of legislative power, and constitutional law, which is made in exercise of constituent power'.[16] The net effect of the Supreme Court's decision in *Shankari Prasad* was that amendments to the Constitution could not be reviewed by courts.

In *Sajjan Singh v. State of Rajasthan* (*Sajjan Singh*),[17] the validity of the Constitution (Seventeenth Amendment) Act, 1964—which inserted forty-four statutes into the Ninth Schedule—was challenged before another five-judge bench of the Supreme Court. Unlike in *Shankari Prasad*, the Parliament's right to amend fundamental rights was not questioned in *Sajjan Singh*. Instead, the case challenged the Parliament's failure to follow the procedure prescribed to amend the Constitution.[18] As was the case in *Shankari Prasad*, this petition was also dismissed unanimously by the judges. However, while three of the five judges agreed that fundamental rights could not be amended, Justices Mohammad Hidayatullah and Janardan Raghunath Mudholkar expressed doubts about the correctness of the view adopted in *Shankari Prasad* that an amendment to the Constitution was not 'law' under Article 13(2) of the Constitution and therefore could not be reviewed by courts. In fact, Justice Mudholkar also sowed the

---

16 *Shankari Prasad v. Union of India*, [1952] 1 SCR 89.

17 AIR 1965 SC 845.

18 H.M. Seervai, *Constitutional Law of India*, 4th ed. (New Delhi: Universal Book Traders, 1999), p. 3110.

seeds for the basic structure doctrine adopted in *Kesavananda* when he referred to the 'intention of the Constituent Assembly to give permanency to the basic features of the Constitution'[19] and said: 'It is also a matter for consideration whether making a change in a basic feature of the Constitution can be regarded merely as an amendment or would it be, in effect, rewriting a part of the Constitution.'[20]

Cordoning Off Fundamental Rights from Constitutional Amendment

Could the Parliament amend fundamental rights? This issue was raised yet again in *I.C. Golak Nath v. State of Punjab* (*Golak Nath*).[21] The petitioners—again, landowners deprived of their surplus landholdings under state land reform legislation—challenged the validity of the First, Fourth and Seventeenth Amendments.[22] The Supreme Court constituted an eleven-judge bench to examine, yet again, whether constitutional amendments could be passed to take away or abridge fundamental rights and whether courts could review such amendments. By a slender majority of 6:5, the Supreme Court ruled that the distinction between constituent power and legislative power laid down in

---

19 *Sajjan Singh v. State of Rajasthan* (AIR 1965 SC 845).

20 Ibid.; also *see* Ramachandran, 'The Supreme Court and the Basic Structure Doctrine', p. 111.

21 AIR 1967 SC 1643.

22 The Constitution (First Amendment) Act, 1951 inserted Articles 31A and 31B into Part III of the Constitution. The Constitution (Fourth Amendment) Act, 1955 amended Article 31A. The Constitution (Seventeenth Amendment) Act, 1964 further amended Article 31A and also included forty-four statutes (almost all dealing with agrarian reforms) in the Ninth Schedule to protect them from judicial review.

Shankari Prasad was unfounded. In other words, constitutional amendments fell within the purview of 'law' under Article 13(2) and courts could review them if they violated the fundamental rights of citizens. The court found fundamental rights to be so sacrosanct and transcendental that even a unanimous vote of all members of the Parliament would not be sufficient to weaken or undermine them.[23]

Though the court asserted that fundamental rights are inviolable, it also admitted that applying this decision across the board to earlier constitutional amendments would lead to chaos, confusion and serious inequities. Therefore, it decided to employ the American doctrine of 'prospective overruling', based on which its decision would apply only to subsequent constitutional amendments. So, the petitioners in *Golak Nath* got no relief, but, in the words of the court in *Kesavananda*, 'left the court with the consolation that posterity will enjoy the fruits of the walnut tree planted by them'![24]

The application of the doctrine of prospective overruling in *Golak Nath* was questionable. To borrow Seervai's words, the doctrine 'had no advocate in Golak Nath's case and it had no defender in Kesavananda's case'.[25] The doctrine's shortcoming is that the court applies a principle to the party before it, but gives the party no relief. All the court can say is that, irrespective of what happens in the case before it, a new rule is laid down for the future—a function that sounds perilously similar to that

---

23　Venkatesh Nayak, 'The Basic Structure of the Indian Constitution', Commonwealth Human Rights Initiative, www.humanrightsinitiative.org/publications/const/the_basic_structure_of_the_indian_constitution.pdf (accessed 31 October 2012).

24　*Kesavananda* at para. 2135.

25　Seervai, *Constitutional Law of India*, p. 3111.

performed by the Parliament. If the court assumes jurisdiction for an exclusively 'future' function as opposed to a 'present–future' jurisdiction, it could be excessively anti-democratic and counter-majoritarian and could damage (what remains of) the democratic balance envisaged in our Constitution. In the United Kingdom, the House of Lords has recognized that prospective overruling amounts to a 'judicial usurpation of the legislative function',[26] while a court of appeal in Canada has stated that 'the most cogent reason for rejecting this technique is the necessity for our courts to maintain their independent, neutral, and non-legislative role'.[27]

In *Golak Nath*, for the first time, the Supreme Court based its decision purely on political philosophy.[28] On legal principles, *Golak Nath* received little acceptance from constitutional scholars. Both academic research and public opinion were driven against the Supreme Court's argument.[29]

Eventually, the Parliament sought to reconcile the question of whether constitutional amendments were 'law' under Article 13 by passing the Constitution (Twenty-fourth Amendment) Act, 1971 and inserting Article 13(4) to expressly exclude constitutional amendments from the ambit of Article 13. Through this amendment, the Parliament nullified the Supreme Court's decision in *Golak Nath* and ensured that amendments to the Constitution could once again not be reviewed by courts even if they violated the fundamental rights of citizens.

26 *National Westminster Bank plc v. Spectrum Plus Limited and Others* ([2005] UKHL 41).

27 *Re Edward and Edward* ((1987) 39 DLR (4th) 654).

28 Das, 'The Supreme Court: An Overview', pp. 19–20.

29 P.K. Tripathi, 'Kesavananda Bharati v. The State of Kerala: Who Wins?', *Supreme Court Cases (Journal)*, vol. 1 (1974): p. 3.

Kesavananda Bharati: The Lead-Up

His Holiness Swami Kesavananda Bharati Sripadagalvaru was the head of Edneer *math*[30] in Kerala. The Kerala Land Reforms Act, 1963 had affected the property of his religious institution, leading him to challenge state land reform legislation in Kerala in 1970.[31] While the proceedings were under way, the Parliament passed the Constitution (Twenty-ninth Amendment) Act, 1972, which inserted certain land reform laws[32] to the Ninth Schedule and adversely affected Swami Kesavananda. Nani Palkhivala, the petitioner's counsel, seized the opportunity and challenged the constitutional validity of the Twenty-fourth, Twenty-fifth and Twenty-ninth Amendments to the Constitution.[33]

Here is a background to each of the amendments that was challenged:

1. According to the Twenty-fourth Amendment (enacted in 1971 to nullify *Golak Nath*), constitutional amendments were not 'law' under Article 13, and the Parliament had the power to amend, vary or repeal any provision of the Constitution.

---

30 A religious establishment (usually Hindu).

31 Arvind Datar, *Commentary on the Constitution of India* (New Delhi: LexisNexis Butterworths Wadhwa Nagpur, 2007), pp. 2021–22.

32 The Kerala Land Reforms (Amendment) Act, 1969 and the Kerala Land Reforms (Amendment) Act, 1971 were inserted into the Ninth Schedule. The Constitution (Twenty-ninth Amendment) Act, 1972, was passed after the Supreme Court struck down the Kerala Land Reforms (Amendment) Act, 1969 in *Kunjukutty Sahib v. State of Kerala* (AIR 1972 SC 2097).

33 Granville Austin, 'The Supreme Court and the Struggle for Custody of the Constitution' in *Supreme But Not Infallible: Essays in Honour of the Supreme Court of India*, eds B.N. Kirpal et al. (New Delhi: Oxford University Press, 2000), p. 6.

2. The Twenty-fifth Amendment (enacted in 1971) gave Articles 39(b) and 39(c)[34]—described by Granville Austin as the most 'classically socialist'[35] provisions in the directive principles of state policy—precedence over the fundamental rights to equality, the seven freedoms[36] and property.[37] It also took away the power of the courts to decide whether a law was actually passed to further the policy laid down in these Articles.

3. The Twenty-ninth Amendment (enacted in 1972) added two land reform statutes to the Ninth Schedule of the Constitution.

The Supreme Court had to reconsider its decisions in *Shankari Prasad*, *Sajjan Singh* and *Golak Nath*. The most critical questions it dealt with were regarding how much amending power was granted to the Parliament under Article 368 and whether that power was unfettered, or could courts review amendments? The petitioners in *Kesavananda* contended that the challenged

---

34 The relevant portion of Article 39 of the Constitution reads: 'The State shall, in particular, direct its policy towards securing . . . (b) that the ownership and control of the material resources of the community are so distributed as best to subserve the common good, (c) that the operation of the economic system does not result in the concentration of wealth and means of production to the common detriment.'

35 Austin, 'The Supreme Court and the Struggle for Custody of the Constitution', p. 5.

36 Article 19 of the Constitution specifies: (i) freedom of speech and expression, (ii) freedom to assemble peaceably without arms, (iii) freedom to form associations or unions, (iv) freedom to move freely throughout India, (v) freedom to reside and settle in any part of India, (vi) freedom to acquire, hold, and dispose of property (subsequently deleted by the Constitution (Forty-fourth Amendment) Act, 1978), and (vii) freedom to practise any profession or to carry on any occupation, trade or business.

37 Set out under Article 31 of the Constitution. A negative duty of the state vis-à-vis the citizen, this is distinct from the freedom enumerated in Article 19(1)(f) of the Constitution, which was a positive right conferred upon the citizen.

amendments nullify some of the most cardinal principles of our Constitution and the Parliament could not draw authority from the Constitution to alter those very principles. On the other hand, the government argued that there was no limit to the Parliament's amending power under Article 368—the Parliament could do anything short of repealing the Constitution itself. Hence, it was relevant for the Supreme Court to examine the Parliament's amending power to ascertain the constitutional validity of the amendments.

Thirteen judges of the Supreme Court sat *en banc*[38] for almost five months to consider questions that stood to define constitutionalism and the exercise of democratic power in India.

'Basic Structure' Doctrine: Judging the Constitutionality of Constitutional Amendments

The court issued as many as eleven separate opinions, with each judge expressing divergent views on every issue, implying that there is no clear indication of what the Supreme Court actually held.[39] For the first time in the court's history, the judges gave a summary of their decision, which four judges refused to sign because they said it was inaccurate![40]

The views of the majority on each issue were as follows:

1. The Twenty-fourth Amendment to the Constitution was valid.

---

38 French term meaning 'on a bench'; used to refer to the hearing of a legal case.

39 M.V. Pylee, *Emerging Trends of Indian Polity* (New Delhi: Regency Publications, 1998), p. 50.

40 Seervai, *Constitutional Law of India*, p. 3112; also *see* T.R. Andhyarujina, 'The Untold Story of How Kesavananda Bharati and the Basic Structure Doctrine Survived an Attempt to Reverse Them by the Supreme Court', *Supreme Court Cases (Journal)*, vol. 9 (2009): p. 33.

2. The Twenty-fifth Amendment to the Constitution was valid, except for the clause ousting the courts' jurisdiction.
3. The Twenty-ninth Amendment to the Constitution was valid.
4. The *Golak Nath* judgement, which had asserted that fundamental rights could not be taken away or nullified by the Parliament, was overruled.
5. There were no implied limitations on the Parliament's power to amend the Constitution under Article 368.

However, the court's most significant decision, made by a thin majority of 7:6, was that although the Parliament had the power to amend any part of the Constitution, it could not use this power to alter or destroy the 'basic structure'—or framework—of the Constitution. In other words, adopting a teleological approach,[41] the Supreme Court held that the expression 'amendment' did not encompass defacing the Constitution such that it lost its identity.[42] All constitutional amendments enacted after the date on which the *Kesavananda* judgement was delivered would have to pass the 'basic-structure filter' created by the Supreme Court. The court empowered itself to judge the constitutionality of amendments and revoke any that compromised the essential features of the Constitution.

And the Basic Features Are . . .

German jurist Professor Dieter Conrad—perhaps influenced by radical constitutional amendments in Germany during the

---

41 S.P. Sathe, *Judicial Activism in India: Transgressing Borders and Enforcing Limits* (New Delhi: Oxford University Press, 2002), p. 78.

42 Nani Palkhivala, *We, the People*, 23rd reprint (New Delhi: UBSPD, 2007), p. 184.

Weimar regime—is responsible for the genesis of the basic structure doctrine.[43] Coming to the judgement of the Supreme Court, there was no unanimity of opinion on what the basic structure was. Each judge in the majority prepared a list of what (according to them) comprised the basic structure—some judges[44] accompanied this with a rider that the list they provided was not exhaustive.

Chief Justice Sikri listed the following features as encompassing the basic structure of the Constitution: supremacy of the Constitution, republican and democratic form of government, secular character of the Constitution, separation of powers between the legislature, executive and judiciary, and the federal character of the Constitution.

Justices Shelat and Grover reproduced, broadly, a similar list, with the following two additional elements: dignity of the individual (secured by fundamental rights) and the mandate to build a welfare state (in the directive principles of state policy), and the unity and integrity of the nation.

Justices Hegde and Mukherjea listed: sovereignty of India, democratic character of India's polity, unity of the country, essential features of the individual freedoms secured to the citizens, and the mandate to build a welfare state and an egalitarian society.

Justice Jagmohan Reddy's basic features comprised: sovereign democratic republic, parliamentary democracy and the three organs of the state.

---

43 Datar, *Commentary on the Constitution of India*, pp. 2022–23.

44 *See*, for example, the judgement of Justices Shelat and Grover in *Kesavananda* in which they stated that the basic features of the Constitution 'cannot be catalogued but can only be illustrated'.

In delineating the basic structure of the Constitution, most judges relied upon the Preamble, the fundamental rights and the directive principles of state policy.[45] It is very difficult to say what these lofty principles constituting the basic structure really mean. The only certainty is that judges will be free to mould the 'basic structure' corpus to emasculate any constitutional amendment that strikes at the 'spirit of Indian democracy'. Upendra Baxi's words in 1974 that *Kesavananda* was 'the Indian Constitution of the future' turned out to be near prophetic.[46]

Observations on the Supreme Court's Judgement in *Kesavananda*

While the Supreme Court's decision in *Golak Nath* was the first significant sign of judicial supremacy in constitutional interpretation, *Kesavananda* firmly established that the Supreme Court was unmatched in authority when it came to constitutional matters. In *Kesavananda*, the Supreme Court made a strategic retreat over amendments to fundamental rights,[47] but significantly broadened the scope of its judicial review by assuming the power to scrutinize all constitutional amendments—not just those affecting fundamental rights. If the Parliament had an unfettered right to amend the Constitution, the Supreme Court had a coextensive power to review and

---

45 Ramachandran, 'The Supreme Court and the Basic Structure Doctrine', p. 115.

46 Upendra Baxi, 'The Constitutional Quicksands of Kesavananda Bharati and the Twenty-Fifth Amendment', *Supreme Court Cases (Journal)*, vol. 1 (1974): p. 45.

47 Richard Stith, 'Unconstitutional Constitutional Amendments: The Extraordinary Power of Nepal's Supreme Court', *The American University Journal of International Law and Policy*, vol. 11 (1996): p. 47.

invalidate any amendment that destroyed its basic structure.[48] To an extent, the majority of judges who recognized the basic structure doctrine in *Kesavananda* sought to achieve a win–win situation for the Parliament and the Supreme Court.

Kesavananda recognizes the distinction between the drafting and the working of the Constitution. Can representative bodies, whose amending power is untrammelled, virtually redraft the Constitution on the pretence of making amendments to it? The Supreme Court answered in the negative. This is significant on issues where the government's stance is anti-majoritarian—where the will of the people's elected representatives does not represent the will of the people. Under the guise of making constitutional amendments, can the Parliament alter the Constitution in a way that is opposed to the nation's most basic values—secularism, representative democracy and independence of the judiciary— even though the people do not want such changes? By limiting the Parliament's power to amend the Constitution, the Supreme Court pre-empted such a scenario and ensured that the people's representatives—meant to be servants of the Constitution— would not become its masters.[49] The decision in *Kesavananda* ensured that the Parliament, which holds its constituent power in trust for the people of India, can never change the fundamental bases of India. The Parliament's power to amend is not limitless and is always coextensive with that of the people.[50]

---

48 *See* also Surya Deva, 'Does the Right to Property Create a Constitutional Tension in Socialist Constitutions: An Analysis with Reference to India and China', *NUJS Law Review*, vol. 1 (2008): p. 583, where the author refers to the 'implied and open-ended limitation (imposed by *Kesavananda*) on the power of Parliament to amend the Constitution'.

49 Palkhivala, *We, the People*, p. 208.

50 Jayadevan, 'Interpretation of the Amending Clause', p. 243.

The basic structure doctrine postulated in *Kesavananda* has been credited with protecting the Indian state from collapsing like many of its South Asian counterparts, whether through totalitarian rule, military coups or other extra-constitutional means.[51] It has also protected India from moving in a 'sharply socialist direction'.[52]

Both *Kesavananda* and *Golak Nath* were decisions taken by a judiciary weary of the Parliament subverting India's constitutional and democratic structure. These decisions were the kind where judges primarily decided on the ends, and then set out to discover the legal means to achieve those predetermined ends. Although Justices Hedge and Mukherjea held that 'no single generation can bind the course of the generation to come', this is what the *Kesavananda* judgement did, in a way. By finding certain parts of the Constitution to be basic, indestructible and immune, even from constitutional amendments, the Supreme Court held that certain parts of the Constitution bound successive parliaments in India in perpetuity. Yet, the power to determine the parts of the Constitution that qualify as 'basic' rests with the Supreme Court, whose interpretation is fluid—the court being a perpetual and indissoluble institution. It is through this interesting arrangement that the stability of basic values is tinged with a little flexibility, and the Supreme Court becomes the safety valve that decides when stability is shaken too much for the well-

---

51 Abhishek Singhvi, 'Emerging India Remarks: India's Constitution and Individual Rights: Diverse Perspectives', *George Washington International Law Review*, vol. 41 (2009): p. 327. *See* Palkhivala, *We, the People*, p. 184—the *Kesavananda* judgement ensured that 'tyranny and despotism' would not 'masquerade as constitutionalism'.

52 Elai Katz, 'On Amending Constitutions: The Legality and Legitimacy of Constitutional Entrenchment', *Columbia Journal of Law and Social Problems*, vol. 29 (1996): p. 251.

being of the nation. It also ensures that the Supreme Court has the final say on what form our Constitution takes at any given point of time, thus giving the Supreme Court the 'custody of the Constitution' and establishing the Supreme Court's supremacy in the realm of the interpretation of the Constitution.

Criticism of the Supreme Court's Verdict

One of the most serious criticisms of *Kesavananda* is that the basic structure doctrine finds no mention in the language of the Constitution[53] and opposes the original intent of the Constituent Assembly. Sathe has even described the judgement as an 'attempt to rewrite the Constitution'.[54] Although some authors have argued that *Kesavananda* is supported by textual constructs,[55] the link between the constitutional text and the basic structure doctrine is very remote. Indeed, the doctrine has very little to do with what is written in the Constitution. The nexus between the doctrine and the Constitution as it has been codified can be attributed more accurately to spirit than to text.

In fact, *Golak Nath* finds more support from the constitutional text than *Kesavananda*. Unlike the case in *Kesavananda*, where the court inferred a power to review constitutional amendments from the basic structure doctrine by holding constitutional amendments as 'law' under Article 13 of the Constitution, the court assumed review jurisdiction[56] through a more

---

53 Kemal Gözler, *Judicial Review of Constitutional Amendments: A Comparative Study* (Bursa: Ekin Press, 2008), p. 9.

54 Sathe, *Judicial Activism in India*, p. 70.

55 Andrew B. Coan, 'The Irrelevance of Writtenness in Constitutional Interpretation', *University of Pennsylvania Law Review*, vol. 158 (2010): p. 1025.

56 Review jurisdiction refers to the jurisdiction of a bench to review its own decision;

direct and textually legitimate (though questionable) route in *Golak Nath*.

Apart from this, *Kesavananda* has been condemned for being too lengthy, thus causing uncertainty about what the eleven opinions collectively mean[57] and what the basic structure actually comprised. The judgement has also been described as one that provides an 'outstanding study on lack of consensus'.[58] The danger with the ambiguity of the basic structure doctrine is that each judge's conception depends on his personal preferences and virtually vests amending power in judges,[59] resting on variable judicial perceptions and majorities.[60]

The basic structure doctrine has also been sharply criticized as being counter-majoritarian, and one that causes a democratic imbalance since it gives inordinate power over constitutional amendments to the Supreme Court,[61] an unelected and self-appointed body. Some have gone to the extent of saying that acts of judicial temerity, such as in *Kesavananda*, can damage democratic principles as much as the totalitarian experiments

---

only the same bench can review the decision on the ground that there is an error apparent on the face of the record.

57 Austin, 'The Supreme Court and the Struggle for Custody of the Constitution', p. 6.

58 Gul Bukhari, 'Resounding Silence', *Daily Times*, 15 November 2010, http://dailytimes.com.pk/default.asp?page=2010%5C11%5C15%5Cstory_15-11-2010_pg3_5 (accessed 20 November 2012).

59 Gözler, *Judicial Review of Constitutional Amendments*, p. 95.

60 Ramachandran, 'The Supreme Court and the Basic Structure Doctrine', p. 129.

61 Madhav Khosla, 'Addressing Judicial Activism in the Indian Supreme Court: Towards an Evolved Debate', *Hastings International and Comparative Law Review*, vol. 32 (2009): p. 55; also *see* Stith, 'Unconstitutional Constitutional Amendments', p. 47, where the author interestingly observed that even though *Kesavananda* was more anti-majoritarian than *Golak Nath*, it received greater public acceptance than the latter.

of Indira Gandhi,[62] although this seems hyperbolic. However, the Supreme Court's message in *Kesavananda* was clear—if any constitutional authority was going to wield substantial power over constitutional interpretation inconsistent with the traditional democratic process, it would be the judiciary.

The Supersession and the Emergency

The then Chief Justice of India, S.M. Sikri was due to retire a day after the decision in *Kesavananda*—on 25 April 1973; the government was yet to announce his successor. As per convention, the senior-most judge of the Supreme Court is generally appointed as the Chief Justice of India; were this convention followed, the Chief Justiceship would have been accorded to Justice Shelat followed by Justices Grover and Hegde. However, angered with the *Kesavananda* decision, the government superseded these three judges who had ruled against it in *Kesavananda*. Instead, it appointed Justice A.N. Ray, who had ruled in its favour, as the Chief Justice of India. This undermined the long-standing practice of appointing the senior-most judges of the Supreme Court. Justices Shelat, Grover and Hegde resigned in protest and the Indira Gandhi government's attempt at muzzling judicial independence in the lead-up to the Emergency began in earnest.

Soon after, Raj Narain, Indira Gandhi's political adversary, challenged her election to the Lok Sabha from the Rae Bareli constituency in the Allahabad High Court. He alleged that Indira Gandhi had committed corrupt practices under the

---

62 Katz, 'On Amending Constitutions', p. 251.

Representation of the People Act, 1951. Accepting this contention, the court voided Indira Gandhi's election. On appeal to the Supreme Court, the judgement of the Allahabad High Court was stayed, and it was held that Indira Gandhi could continue to function as the Prime Minister of India on the condition that she would not draw a salary and would not speak or vote in the Parliament. The fallout of this judgement was that a national Emergency was proclaimed in India[63] on 25 June 1975. It lasted twenty-one months.

During the pendency of the appeal, the Parliament hurriedly passed the Constitution (Thirty-ninth Amendment) Act, 1975, placing the election of the President, Vice-President, Prime Minister and Speaker of the Lok Sabha beyond the scrutiny of courts. The amendment was meant to nullify the judgement of the Allahabad High Court so as to shield Indira Gandhi's election from being challenged in the Supreme Court. As a result, in *Indira Nehru Gandhi v. Raj Narain*,[64] Raj Narain challenged the validity of the constitutional amendment itself—the first time a constitutional amendment was challenged not in respect of the right to property or social welfare, but with reference to an electoral law.[65] By a majority of 4:1, the Supreme Court struck down the amendment, recognizing that it vitiated certain fundamental tenets forming part of the basic structure of the Constitution, including free and fair elections and the rule of law. Although four of the five judges had not accepted the basic structure argument in *Kesavananda*, they recognized that they

---

63   Andhyarujina, 'The Untold Story of How Kesavananda Bharati and the Basic Structure Doctrine Survived', p. 33.

64   AIR 1975 SC 2299.

65   Seervai, *Constitutional Law of India*, p. 3117.

were bound by the decision and applied the theory in this case. However, Indira Gandhi's election was not affected, since the court upheld retrospective amendments to the electoral laws.

The Unsuccessful Attempt to Review *Kesavananda*

In 1975, in the midst of the national Emergency declared by the Indira Gandhi-led Congress government, the Chief Justice of India A.N. Ray constituted a thirteen-judge bench to review the Supreme Court's decision in *Kesavananda*. The bench was dissolved after two days of hearings and much of what transpired was shrouded in secrecy. The reporting of courts' judgements by the press was also restricted at the time.[66] Only those lawyers and judges who were present in the courtroom at that time, therefore, could give accounts of what had occurred.

Austin has described this disintegration of the bench (which was to review *Kesavananda*) as 'the most critical moment' for the Constitution and Supreme Court since the original decision in *Kesavananda*.[67] One of the principal arguments for the review of *Kesavananda* was that the basic structure doctrine was nebulous, and every judge had different opinions about what the doctrine encompassed.[68] The Supreme Court rightly chose uncertain democracy over certain tyranny.

---

66 Andhyarujina, 'The Untold Story of How Kesavananda Bharati and the Basic Structure Doctrine Survived', p. 33.

67 Austin, 'The Supreme Court and the Struggle for Custody of the Constitution', p. 8.

68 Andhyarujina, 'The Untold Story of How Kesavananda Bharati and the Basic Structure Doctrine Survived', p. 33.

The Last Effort at Parliamentary Supremacy

During the Emergency, the Parliament passed the most controversial and revolutionary of the constitutional amendments—the Constitution (Forty-second Amendment) Act, 1976 (the Forty-second Amendment Act). Enacted to eliminate 'impediments to the growth of the Constitution',[69] the amendment virtually remoulded the original Constitution through sweeping changes—substantive and symbolic—such as: the insertion of Part IVA into the Constitution, which highlighted the 'fundamental duties' of citizens, enabling the protection of any laws that gave effect to the directive principles under Article IV of the Constitution, insertion of the expressions 'socialist' and 'secular' into the Preamble to the Constitution, amendment of Article 368 nullifying the decision in *Kesavananda* that the Parliament's amending power was subject to the 'basic structure' limitation, and strengthening the position of the Central government vis-à-vis the state governments. This amendment was a manifestation of India's distinct shift to the political left.

Within a couple of years of the Forty-second Amendment Act being passed, the owners of a textile mill in Karnataka challenged the government's nationalization of their undertaking. The mill was nationalized under a statute placed in the Ninth Schedule by the Parliament. In *Minerva Mills v. Union of India* (*Minerva Mills*),[70] the petitioners challenged the validity of Section 55 of the Forty-second Amendment Act, which amended Article

---

69 Statement of Objects and Reasons appended to the Constitution (Forty-second Amendment) Act, 1976.

70 AIR 1980 SC 1789.

368 to transform the Parliament's amending power over the Constitution (which was limited by *Kesavananda*) into an unlimited one. The Supreme Court unanimously struck down the amendments to Article 368, holding that judicial review and a limited amending power were basic features of the Constitution, which, according to the judgement in *Kesavananda*, could not be altered, destroyed or nullified. The court's logic was simple—if a donee was vested with limited power, it could not be permitted to exercise that very power and convert it into an unlimited one.[71] To take the aid of a simple example, if a genie grants you three wishes, it is understood that you cannot, as one of your wishes, ask for an unlimited number of wishes!

The Supreme Court's judgement in *Minerva Mills* established that from the perspective of the basic structure doctrine, a minimum standard of judicial review was inviolate.[72] *Minerva Mills* was the last case in which the government made a concerted effort to establish parliamentary supremacy over the Constitution.[73] Having failed to scale back on the basic structure doctrine, *Minerva Mills* marks the beginning of an era of judicial supremacy in India, with the Supreme Court firmly entrenched as the final arbiter of constitutional interpretation in India.

The Ninth Schedule and Judicial Review

Since the insertion of the Ninth Schedule into the Constitution in 1951, 284 statutes (or segments) have come under its

---

71 Palkhivala, *We, the People*, p. 210.

72 Krishnamurthy, 'Colonial Cousins: Explaining India and Canada's Unwritten Constitutional Principles', p. 207.

73 Ramachandran, 'The Supreme Court and the Basic Structure Doctrine', p. 108.

protection. Although it was initially meant to protect land reform legislation, the schedule now contains many statutes that have little to do with land reform—the Essential Commodities Act, 1955, the Levy Sugar Price Equalisation Fund Act, 1976, and the Bonded Labour System (Abolition) Act, 1976 to cite a few examples. In many cases, statutes or provisions of statutes which were struck down as violating fundamental rights could be protected by inserting them into the Ninth Schedule through constitutional amendments.[74]

The critical question before a nine-judge bench of the Supreme Court in *I.R. Coelho v. State of Tamil Nadu* (*Coelho*)[75] was whether after the date of the *Kesavananda* decision, statutes could be made exempt from the test of satisfying fundamental rights by their insertion into the Ninth Schedule. The Supreme Court held that while laws could be added to the Ninth Schedule, once Article 32 (the right to move the Supreme Court for the enforcement of fundamental rights) was triggered, they would be subjected to the test of fundamental rights, which were a part of the basic structure. The court also asserted that if any legislation added to the Ninth Schedule sought to nullify the principles of the 'golden triangle'[76] of fundamental rights, it would be declared void. Therefore, all amendments seeking to insert

---

74 *See*, for instance, the Gudalur Janmam Estates (Abolition and Conversion into Ryotwari) Act, 1969 which was struck down by the Supreme Court in *Balmadies Plantations Ltd. v. State of Tamil Nadu* ([1973] 1 SCR 258) and later inserted in the Ninth Schedule by the Constitution (Thirty-fourth Amendment) Act, 1974.

75 AIR 2007 SC 861.

76 This includes: (i) the right to equality before the law and the equal protection of the laws (Article 14 of the Constitution), (ii) the protection of the six freedoms—originally seven till the right to property under Article 19(1)(f) of the Constitution was deleted—of citizens (Article 19 of the Constitution), and (iii) the right to life and personal liberty (Article 21 of the Constitution).

legislation into the Ninth Schedule would be subjected to a two-fold test: (1) Did they conform with the basic structure of the Constitution? and (2) Did they conform with the fundamental rights as forming a part of the basic structure under Part III of the Constitution? The second test is a natural corollary of the first. The court unanimously concluded that the government could not wantonly exploit the Ninth Schedule as the 'black hole' of the Constitution.

Apart from marking a significant development in the Supreme Court's basic structure jurisprudence,[77] *Coelho* has preserved the supremacy of the judiciary in constitutional adjudication.

Has the Basic Structure Doctrine Outlived Its Purpose?

A hotly contested question among scholars of constitutional law is whether the basic structure doctrine, formulated at the height of an oppressive era of single-party dominance, has crossed its expiry date. In the era of coalition politics, it is very unlikely that any party will wield the power that the Indira Gandhi government exercised in the 1970s. Yet, if one had to choose between the legislature and the judiciary as the custodian of the Constitution, it would likely be the latter.

Although the *Kesavananda* decision does not find favour with those who have been brought up with the traditional concept of judicial review, even sceptics would admit that it was the judiciary's rescue operation that saved Indian democracy.[78] From a practical perspective, arguments against the basic structure doctrine have been largely speculative, based on how some useful

---

77   Khosla, 'Addressing Judicial Activism in the Indian Supreme Court', p. 55.

78   Jayadevan, 'Interpretation of the Amending Clause', p. 243.

structural changes would be vitiated by its operation. Although authors have opined on the possible evils of the doctrine, it has not stalled any beneficial constitutional amendment so far and Indian courts have invoked it sparingly. Have we learnt from our mistakes? Unless we can say with conviction that we have, there is no saying that history will not repeat itself.

A hypothetical question before we close this chapter: if we accept the argument of those who oppose the basic structure doctrine, how can we discard it? Since the system of binding precedents in India rests on the principle of law that a judgement represents a decision of the entire bench of judges (not only those in the majority), another bench consisting of at least thirteen judges would have to be constituted to reconsider *Kesavananda*.[79] Moreover, since *Kesavananda*, by its very nature, cannot be overruled by the legitimate exercise of legislative power, the only other method of doing so would be through extra-constitutional means. Both of these situations seem highly improbable, at least in the near future. In any event, as a safety valve to preserve Indian democracy, the basic structure doctrine in *Kesavananda* should live on.

---

79 Chintan Chandrachud, 'The Supreme Court's Practice of Referring Cases to Larger Benches: A Need for Review', *Supreme Court Cases (Journal)*, vol. 1 (2010): p. 37.

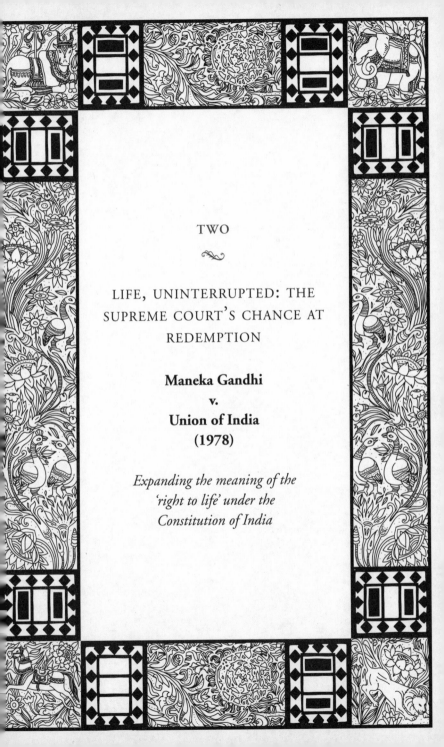

TWO

LIFE, UNINTERRUPTED: THE
SUPREME COURT'S CHANCE AT
REDEMPTION

Maneka Gandhi
v.
Union of India
(1978)

*Expanding the meaning of the
'right to life' under the
Constitution of India*

THE DECISION OF the Supreme Court of India in *Maneka Gandhi v. Union of India*[1] (*Maneka Gandhi*) was an 'inflexion point'[2] in the court's movement towards a broader interpretation of the fundamental rights guaranteed by the Constitution.

The circumstances that set the stage for the *Maneka Gandhi* judgement in 1978 are important. The national Emergency, which was declared by President Fakhruddin Ali Ahmed in 1975 and was characterized by strict censorship and detention of political prisoners, had recently ended.[3] In 1976, in the case of *ADM Jabalpur v. Shivkant Shukla*[4] (*ADM Jabalpur*), the Supreme Court had unhappily held that a detenu could not file a habeas corpus petition[5] challenging the legality of his detention during an emergency. A large segment of citizens had lost faith in the judiciary. India's democratic structure had faced an onslaught, as the Indira Gandhi-led Congress government (ousted in 1977) had passed a deluge of revolutionary constitutional amendments which severely impinged on a person's fundamental rights.

---

1   AIR 1978 SC 597.
2   Adam M. Smith, 'Making Itself at Home—Understanding Foreign Law in Domestic Jurisprudence: The Indian Case', *Berkeley Journal of International Law*, vol. 24 (2006): p. 218.
3   The Emergency lasted twenty-one months—from 25 June 1975 to 21 March 1977.
4   AIR 1976 SC 1207.
5   A petition filed under Article 32 of the Constitution seeking the release of a person from the unlawful custody of the state.

There was an air of disillusionment among the people, who felt betrayed by their elected representatives and abandoned by the highest court of the land.

With its decision in *Maneka Gandhi*, the Supreme Court attempted to restore the citizens' faith in the judiciary. It went beyond its immediate mandate to make some striking assertions, which went on to become the bedrock of the protection of human rights of the *aam aadmi*[6] in the years that followed.[7] The case marked the beginning of a golden era of human rights jurisprudence in India[8]—a period in which the Supreme Court transformed itself into an 'institutional ombudsman of human rights'.[9]

Scheme of Fundamental Rights, Article 21 and the Due Process Clause

The impact of the *Maneka Gandhi* case can be seen in the backdrop of constitutional provisions, which the Supreme Court was called upon to interpret on several occasions until its decision in *Maneka Gandhi* in 1978. Part III of the Constitution of India, dealing with fundamental rights, is arguably its most significant component, for two reasons: (1) Any law that abridges

---

6 Commonly used term in India; translated from the Hindi to mean 'the common man'.

7 It is ironic that the case involved the right to travel abroad of the daughter-in-law of former Prime Minister Indira Gandhi. *See* Laurence H. Tribe and Patrick O. Gudridge, 'The Anti-Emergency Constitution', *Yale Law Journal*, vol. 113 (2004): p. 1801.

8 Ibid.

9 Fali Nariman, 'The "Doctrine" versus "Majoritarianism"' in *The Supreme Court versus the Constitution: A Challenge to Federalism*, ed. Pran Chopra (New Delhi: Sage Publications, 2006), p. 94.

or takes away the rights conferred under Part III is void,[10] and (2) Every person is entitled to approach the Supreme Court directly to enforce his/her fundamental rights under Part III.[11]

Amongst the fundamental rights, Articles 14, 19 and 21 of the Constitution—composing the 'golden triangle'[12]—have been invoked most often to declare legislation or arbitrary state action invalid.

Article 14 categorically sets out that the state cannot deny to any person equality before the law or the equal protection of laws in India.

Article 19 grants the following six freedoms[13] to all citizens of India (subject to certain restrictions): (1) The freedom of speech and expression, (2) The freedom to assemble peaceably and without arms, (3) The freedom to form associations or unions, (4) The freedom to move freely throughout the territory of India, (5) The freedom to reside and settle in any part of the territory of India, and (6) The freedom to practise any profession, or to carry on any occupation, trade or business.

The right to life and personal liberty under Article 21 reads: 'No person shall be deprived of his life or personal liberty except according to procedure established by law.' The phrase 'procedure established by law' was the subject of profound debate in the Constituent Assembly at the time of the formulation of the Indian Constitution—would the deprivation of a citizen's life

---

10 Article 13 of the Constitution.

11 Article 32 of the Constitution.

12 *I.R. Coelho v. State of Tamil Nadu* (AIR 2007 SC 861); *Minerva Mills Ltd. v. Union of India* (AIR 1980 SC 1789).

13 Article 19 of the Constitution originally contained seven freedoms. However, the freedom to 'acquire, hold and dispose of property' under Article 19(1)(f) was deleted by the Constitution (Forty-fourth Amendment) Act, 1978.

or personal liberty be undertaken under 'procedure established by law' or under 'due process of law'?[14]

Eventually, the Constituent Assembly retained the expression 'procedure established by law' as a part of Article 21. Our founding fathers intended for courts to examine only the procedural adequacy of laws under Article 21. In other words, courts were not allowed to question any law—no matter how arbitrary or oppressive—as violating the right to life or personal liberty if the law had been suitably passed and enacted. Indeed, most members of the Constituent Assembly believed that only the electorate should wield the power of substantive appraisal of legislation.

A 'Positivist' Supreme Court: *Gopalan* and *Satwant Singh*

In 1950, for the first time, the Supreme Court was asked to interpret fundamental rights under the Constitution in

---

14 Some scholars believed that the American expression 'due process of law' ought to have replaced the phrase 'procedure established by law' (borrowed from Japan). Other members of the Drafting Committee, led by its constitutional advisor Sir B.N. Rau, felt that the inclusion of the 'due process clause' was ill-advised. The distinction between 'procedure established by law' and 'due process of law' is that while the former was intended to permit courts to question laws merely on procedural irregularities, the latter allowed judges to delve into the merits and substance of the law as well. Naturally, a due process clause tilts the democratic balance of power between the judiciary and the legislature in favour of the courts. Sir Rau held discussions with several legal experts including Justice Felix Frankfurter (a distinguished judge of the Supreme Court of the United States of America) and concluded that the inclusion of a due process clause would be 'undemocratic and burdensome to the judiciary' (*see* Madhav Khosla, 'Addressing Judicial Activism in the Indian Supreme Court: Towards an Evolved Debate', *Hastings International and Comparative Law Review*, vol. 32 (2009): p. 55). The framers of our Constitution were also concerned about the fact that social welfare legislation was being consistently invalidated by the Supreme Court of the United States of America, based on the due process clause in the United States Constitution (*see* Martha C. Nussbaum, 'India: Implementing Sex Equality Through Law', *Chicago Journal of International Law*, vol. 2 (2001): p. 35).

A.K. Gopalan v. State of Madras[15] (*Gopalan*). The petitioner, a social and political worker (who later became the first leader of the Opposition in Parliament), filed a habeas corpus petition seeking his release from detention under the Preventive Detention Act, 1950. He claimed that the said act violated Articles 13,[16] 19,[17] 21[18] and 22[19] of the Constitution and therefore the Madras government's order of preventive detention was illegal.

The petitioner said that each of the cited fundamental rights were to be read collectively, in tandem. The Supreme Court disagreed, holding that the fundamental rights dealt with distinct matters and should be considered in isolation. What this implied was that when a law meets the requirements of the fundamental right applying to it, it cannot be said that the law is against any other fundamental right.[20] In *Gopalan*, the court held that since the conditions set out in Article 22 (which encompasses the safeguards against preventive detention) had been satisfied, the petitioner was not entitled to challenge his detention under any other fundamental right, such as the right to life and personal liberty under Article 21. The court also refused to acknowledge any similarity between the American 'due process clause' and the

---

15 AIR 1950 SC 27.

16 Article 13 sets out that laws that take away or abridge fundamental rights are void.

17 Article 19 of the Constitution encompasses, as discussed before, the protection of certain rights regarding freedom of speech, etc.

18 Article 21 of the Constitution sets out the right to life and personal liberty.

19 Article 22 of the Constitution contains the constitutional safeguards against arrest and detention.

20 Vijayashri Sripati, 'Freedom from Torture and Cruel, Inhuman or Degrading Treatment or Punishment: The Role of the Supreme Court of India' in *Judicial Protection of Human Rights: Myth or Reality*, eds Stanislaw Frankowski and Mark Gibney (Westport: Praeger, 1999), p. 109.

expression 'procedure established by law' found in Article 21; in fact, it specifically pointed out marked differences between the two.[21]

In *Gopalan*, the majority opinion was based on what it perceived as the original and historical intent of the Constitution.[22] Sathe has described the court's stand in *Gopalan* as 'extremely positivist' and one that 'gave finality to the law enacted by the legislature'.[23] People ascribe the decision in *Gopalan* to the pressures on the Supreme Court at the time. The Constitution had been adopted very recently by the Constituent Assembly (which was still acting as the interim Parliament at the time the *Gopalan* decision was delivered), and therefore the judges would have been wary of disturbing the Assembly's understanding of the Constitution. The constitutional history of the due process clause and its express rejection would have weighed heavily on their minds.

The *Maneka Gandhi* case concerned the fundamental right of an Indian citizen to travel abroad. It was not the first judgement on the subject; there was a conflict of opinion among different

---

21   The court highlighted the differences between the United States Constitution's 'due process clause' and Article 21 of the Indian Constitution: (i) In the US Constitution the word 'liberty' is used simply (in the ordinary sense of the term), while in India, it is restricted to personal liberty, (ii) under the US Constitution the same protection is given to property while in India the fundamental right in respect of property is contained in a different provision—Article 31 (later repealed by the Constitution (Forty-fourth Amendment) Act, 1978), (iii) the word 'due' is omitted altogether and the expression 'due process of law' is deliberately not used in the Indian Constitution, and (iv) the word 'established' is used and is qualified by the term 'procedure' under the Indian Constitution.

22   Manoj Mate, 'The Origins of Due Process in India: The Role of Borrowing in Personal Liberty and Preventive Detention Cases', *Berkeley Journal of International Law*, vol. 28 (2010): p. 216.

23   S.P. Sathe, *Judicial Activism in India: Transgressing Borders and Enforcing Limits* (New Delhi: Oxford University Press, 2002), p. 52.

high courts in the country on whether the right to travel abroad formed a part of the right to personal liberty under Article 21.[24] This conflict was resolved by the Supreme Court in *Satwant Singh v. Assistant Passport Officer, Government of India*[25] (*Satwant Singh*).

In *Satwant Singh*, the petitioner was a manufacturer, importer and exporter of automobile parts and engineering goods. His business involved regular overseas travel. The external affairs ministry asked him to surrender his passports on the ground that he was likely to leave India to avoid a trial he was expected to face, for offences under laws governing imports and exports. He moved the Supreme Court, contending that the state's actions violated his fundamental rights under Articles 14 and 21.

The Supreme Court concluded that the expression 'liberty' under Article 21 had a wide import and excluded only what was otherwise expressly protected under Article 19. The majority on the bench followed the decision in *Gopalan* by treating the fundamental rights under Articles 14, 19 and 21 as distinct from one another. The court recognized that the right to life and personal liberty could be taken away by a 'procedure established by law'. However, it cancelled the government's order to the petitioner to surrender his passports. Its judgement was founded on the limited ground of the failure to provide for any procedure regulating the denial/surrender of passports under the Indian

---

24   *See*, for example, the decision of the Delhi High Court in *Rabindernath Malik v. The Regional Passport Officer, New Delhi* (AIR 1967 Del 1) which held that 'personal liberty' did not include the liberty to travel outside India; and the Mysore High Court's judgement in *Dr. S.S. Sadashiva Rao v. Union of India* ([1965] 2 Mys. LJ 605) (Karnataka High Court), which asserted that Article 21 of the Constitution encompassed the right to travel abroad and return to India.

25   AIR 1967 SC 1836.

Passport Act, 1920 (the law governing passports at the time). The court's objection was based on the absence of a procedure rather than the merits of an existing system.[26] Soon after the *Satwant Singh* judgement, the Parliament enacted the Passports Act, 1967 (the Passports Act) to regulate how passports would be issued, refused, impounded and/or revoked—matters on which comprehensive legislation did not exist earlier.

The Impounding of Maneka Gandhi's Passport

The *Maneka Gandhi* case arose in the period immediately following the end of the national Emergency in India, with the Janata Party government assuming power in 1977. Maneka Gandhi, daughter-in-law of former Prime Minister Indira Gandhi and founder-editor of a political magazine *Surya*, was issued a passport in 1976 under the Passports Act. Soon after the Congress Party was ousted by the Janata Party, she began using *Surya* as a political platform to restore the image of the Congress Party and discredit leaders of the new government. (The most notable instance of this was when *Surya* carried photographs showing the son of then defence minister Jagjivan Ram engaging in sexual intercourse with a student of Delhi University.) In 1977, around the time she wished to leave India to fulfil a speaking engagement,[27] Maneka Gandhi received a letter stating that the Government of India had decided to impound her passport 'in

---

26 S.P. Sathe, 'Judicial Activism: The Indian Experience', *Washington University Journal of Law and Policy*, vol. 6 (2001): p. 29.

27 Anthony Lester QC, 'The Overseas Trade in the American Bill of Rights', *Columbia Law Review*, vol. 88 (1988): p. 537.

public interest' under Section 10(3)(c)[28] of the Passports Act. The government turned down her request seeking the reasons why the order had been passed, stating that it was not 'in the interest of the general public'.[29] In reaction, she filed a writ petition in the Supreme Court challenging the passport impounding order of the Government of India and its subsequent refusal to provide reasons for the same.

Breathing Life into Article 21

Before discussing the Supreme Court's decision in *Maneka Gandhi*, it is important to note that the rigid approach adopted by the Supreme Court in *Gopalan*—holding that: (1) Each fundamental right is distinct and must be read in isolation, and (2) The expression 'personal liberty' under Article 21 excludes those freedoms that are categorically provided for in Article 19—had been significantly diluted in two cases[30] decided by the Supreme Court in the pre-Emergency era. These cases were extensively cited in the judgement of the Supreme Court in *Maneka Gandhi*.

---

28 The section states: 'The passport authority may impound or cause to be impounded or revoke a passport or travel document ... (c) if the passport authority deems it necessary so to do in the interests of the sovereignty and integrity of India, the security of India, friendly relations of India with any foreign country, or in the interests of the general public.'

29 It was later discovered that the primary reason for the government's decision to impound Maneka Gandhi's passport was its fear that she would flee India to avoid giving testimony to a Commission of Inquiry set up to investigate crimes committed during the Emergency (involving her husband) (*see* Manoj Mate, 'The Origins of Due Process in India: The Role of Borrowing in Personal Liberty and Preventive Detention Cases', *Berkeley Journal of International Law*, vol. 28 (2010): p. 216).

30 *Kharak Singh v. State* of *U.P.* (AIR 1963 SC 1295); *R.C. Cooper v. Union of India* (AIR 1970 SC 1318).

In *Maneka Gandhi*, the Supreme Court departed from the straitjacketed interpretation of fundamental rights in *Gopalan* and held that the fundamental rights form an integrated scheme under the Constitution. The court stated:

> Articles dealing with different fundamental rights contained in Part III of the Constitution do not represent entirely separate streams of rights which do not mingle at many points. They are all parts of an integrated scheme in the Constitution. Their waters must mix to constitute that grand flow of unimpeded and impartial justice . . . Isolation of various aspects of human freedom, for purposes of their protection, is neither realistic nor beneficial.[31]

Emphasizing the need to read Part III of the Constitution in a holistic manner, the Supreme Court said that the mere fact that a law satisfied the requirements of one fundamental right did not exempt it from the operation of other fundamental rights. What this means is that even if a law were ostensibly associated with a particular fundamental right and complied with its requirements, it would also have to satisfy the requirements of other fundamental rights.

The majority on the seven-judge bench stated that any procedure established by law under Article 21 would have to be 'fair, just and reasonable' and could not be 'fanciful, oppressive or arbitrary'.[32] If this standard were applied, the government's impounding order—passed without providing a hearing nor furnishing any reasons to Maneka Gandhi—failed to satisfy

31 *Maneka Gandhi* at para. 3.
32 Ibid., para. 40.

the mandate of Article 21. The court affirmed the decision in *Satwant Singh* and held that the right to travel abroad fell within the sweep of the right to personal liberty under Article 21. The court also found that the government order was arbitrary and violated the right to equality under Article 14.

In spite of its emphatic observations, the court did not pass any 'formal order' in the case and accepted the government's assurance that Maneka Gandhi would get an adequate opportunity to be heard.[33] The majority upheld the impounding of Maneka Gandhi's passport and held that her passport should remain in the court's custody in the meantime. Justice Beg, who was otherwise part of the majority, did opine that the government order was 'neither fair nor procedurally proper' and deserved to be quashed by the court.[34]

Small Case, Large Judgement?

The Supreme Court's judgement in *Maneka Gandhi* has been widely critiqued as one that went out of bounds with reference to the facts before the court. The matter concerned, on the face of it, the impounding of an individual's passport. The Attorney-General had undertaken that Maneka Gandhi would be provided a post-decisional hearing. Moreover, even if the government decided to stand by its impounding order after hearing Maneka Gandhi, it had conceded that the period of impounding would not exceed six months from the date of its fresh order. Instead of deciding the case on this finite ground, the court chose to

---

33 Seervai's criticism of the final order in *Maneka Gandhi* as being self-contradictory makes for an interesting read. *See* H.M. Seervai, *Constitutional Law of India*, 3rd ed. (Bombay: N.M. Tripathi, 1984), p. 2094.

34 *Maneka Gandhi* at para. 38.

consider several peripheral issues—yes, these issues were pivotal to India's governance, but peripheral to the case—in judgements that together added up to over 70,000 words. In his candid style, constitutional scholar Arvind Datar said: '[t]here was really no need to write pages after pages on Articles 14, 19, 21 and so on.'[35]

Indeed, why did the Supreme Court say more than what needed to be said? The immediate cause of the court's expansive, rights-based approach in *Maneka Gandhi* was the criticism it faced for its decision during the Emergency in *ADM Jabalpur*. In fact, *Maneka Gandhi* was followed by a series of actions undertaken by the court and its judges to distance themselves from *ADM Jabalpur*—this was akin to an acknowledgement that it had 'violated the fundamental rights of a large number of people'[36] thirty-four years after the case was decided.

And, yet, though the Supreme Court embarked on an inquiry not necessitated by the facts before it in *Maneka Gandhi*, when we look at it from a result-oriented approach, the court's interpretation of Articles 14, 19 and 21 played a hugely beneficial role in shaping India's constitutional policy.

The Due Process Clause Gets Its Visa to India

Does a law that satisfies all procedural requirements in its enactment, however arbitrary or unreasonable, meet the test of Article 21? This is the question that the Supreme Court sought

---

35 Arvind Datar, *Commentary on the Constitution of India* (New Delhi: LexisNexis Butterworths Wadhwa Nagpur, 2007), p. 64. Also, *see* Seervai, *Constitutional Law of India*, p. 2089, where Seervai opined that it was not necessary for the Supreme Court to engage in an 'elaborate discussion' on personal liberty—even if the expression were narrowly construed, preventing a person from leaving the country would fall within its ambit.

36 *Remdeo Chauhan v. Bani Kant Das* (AIR 2011 SC 615).

to answer in *Maneka Gandhi*. By vesting in itself the power of substantive review under Article 21, the court transformed itself from being merely a supervisor, to being a watchdog of the Constitution. This is the seminal importance of the *Maneka Gandhi* decision.

The key difference between *Satwant Singh* and *Maneka Gandhi* was that, in the former, the court objected to the restraint on travelling abroad because of the absence of a law, but it did so in the latter despite the existence of a law. The court's judgement in *Maneka Gandhi* is based on the simple premise that an arbitrary law is no law.

Although the makers of the Constitution rejected the American due process clause, the Supreme Court's judgement in *Maneka Gandhi* effectively meant that 'procedure established by law' under Article 21 would have the same effect as the expression 'due process of law'. In a subsequent decision,[37] the Supreme Court stated that Article 21, interpreted according to *Maneka Gandhi*, would read as: 'No person shall be deprived of his life or personal liberty except according to *fair, just and reasonable* procedure established by *valid* law'.

Maneka Gandhi is a reflection of dynamic constitutional interpretation. It signifies the court's changing approach towards the Constitution. In the decades that followed, it was treated as an organic document whose interpretation must evolve with the times. Substantive due process and, more broadly stated, the court's power to review the content of legislation to ascertain if the mandate of Article 21 had been met, eventually found its way to India more than twenty-eight years after the founding fathers of our Constitution abandoned it.

---

37 *Bachan Singh v. State of Punjab* (AIR 1980 SC 898).

An Altered Constitutional Climate

Some would wonder why there was so much excitement over a verdict that essentially recognized the right of a member of India's most influential political family to go abroad. It is the constitutional developments after *Maneka Gandhi* that highlight how it was one of the cases that truly changed India. For most jurists, it was a turning point in the Supreme Court's interpretation of Article 21. The court moved from a pedantic to a purposive approach in construing the sweep of the right to life under the Constitution. The judgement became a springboard for the evolution of the law relating to judicial preservation of human rights.[38]

The most striking aspect of the Supreme Court's introduction of substantive due process was that it empowered courts to expand the limited phraseology of the right to life under the Constitution, to include a wide range of un-enumerated rights.[39] Derived from Article 21, these rights cover areas such as the rights of prisoners, protection of women and children, and environmental rights. Since *Maneka Gandhi*, courts have included the following rights[40] within the embrace of the right to life and personal liberty under Article 21:

1. **Rights of Prisoners** including protection from handcuffing without adequate reasons,[41] access to a transcript of the judgement and facilities to exercise his right to appeal

---

38 Nariman, 'The "Doctrine" versus "Majoritarianism"', p. 94.

39 Vikram Raghavan, 'Navigating the Noteworthy and Nebulous in Naz Foundation', *National University of Juridical Sciences Law Review*, vol. 2 (2009): p. 397.

40 The enumerated rights are for illustration and are by no means exhaustive.

41 *Prem Shankar Shukla v. Delhi Administration* (AIR 1980 SC 1535).

against his conviction,[42] the right to treatment with dignity and humanity,[43] the right of an undertrial to be released from custody if the police fail to file a chargesheet within the period prescribed by law,[44] protection from custodial violence[45] and protection against public hanging.[46]

2. **Environmental Rights** including the right to a humane and healthy environment,[47] the right to sustainable development,[48] protection from pollution hazards due to use of pesticides,[49] and the right to live without undue affection of air, water and the environment[50]

3. **Other Rights** including the right to live with human dignity, including access to nutrition, clothing, and shelter,[51] the right to free education of children up to the age of fourteen years,[52] the right to livelihood,[53] protection of one's reputation,[54] access to just and humane conditions of work, protection of the health and strength of workers and maternity relief.[55]

---

42 *Hoskot v. State of Maharashtra* (AIR 1978 SC 1548).

43 *Sunil Batra v. Delhi Administration* (AIR 1980 SC 1565).

44 *Hussainara Khatoon v. State of Bihar* (AIR 1979 SC 1360).

45 *Sheela Barse v. State of Maharashtra* (AIR 1983 SC 378).

46 *Attorney General of India v. Lachma Devi* (AIR 1986 SC 467).

47 *Godavarman Thirumalpad v. Union of India* (AIR 2003 SC 724).

48 *N.D. Jayal v. Union of India* (AIR 2004 SC 867).

49 *Ashok v. Union of India* (AIR 1997 SC 2298).

50 *Rural Litigation and Environment Kendra v. State of Uttar Pradesh* (AIR 1985 SC 652).

51 *Francis Coralie Mullin v. Union Territory of Delhi* (AIR 1981 SC 746).

52 *Unni Krishnan v. State of Andhra Pradesh* (AIR 1993 SC 2178).

53 *Olga Tellis v. Bombay Municipal Corporation* (AIR 1986 SC 180).

54 *Board of Trustees for Port of Bombay v. Dilipkumar Nadkarni* (AIR 1983 SC 109).

55 *Bandhua Mukti Morcha v. Union of India* (AIR 1984 SC 802).

The Lasting Impact of *Maneka Gandhi*

Although the *Maneka Gandhi* judgement permanently clipped the wings of the legislature, it faced little or no hostility from any of the branches of the government,[56] unlike other judgements in the same period. In over three decades since the judgement, the right to life and personal liberty under Article 21 has gradually become a repository of human rights and fundamental freedoms in India.[57]

---

56 Khosla, 'Addressing Judicial Activism in the Indian Supreme Court', p. 55.

57 *See*, for instance, the political opposition to the decisions of the Supreme Court in *Kesavananda Bharati v. State of Kerala* (AIR 1973 SC 1461) and *Mohammed Ahmed Khan v. Shah Bano Begum* (AIR 1985 SC 945).

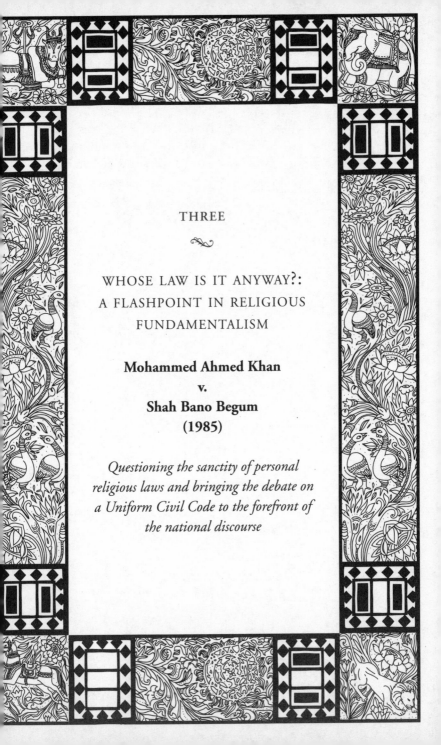

THREE

WHOSE LAW IS IT ANYWAY?:
A FLASHPOINT IN RELIGIOUS
FUNDAMENTALISM

Mohammed Ahmed Khan

v.

Shah Bano Begum

(1985)

*Questioning the sanctity of personal
religious laws and bringing the debate on
a Uniform Civil Code to the forefront of
the national discourse*

Introduction

IN APRIL 1985, the Supreme Court delivered a judgement on the maintenance a divorced Muslim woman would be entitled to receive from her former husband in the case of *Mohammed Ahmed Khan v. Shah Bano Begum*[1] (*Shah Bano*). It was not a unique case; in fact, it was rather ubiquitous—the very same court had judged similar cases earlier. And yet, the Shah Bano case was different. The circumstances of the case, the manner in which the court formulated its verdict and the publicity that it received altered the communal climate in India for all time to come.[2]

Although it was the decision of a court, the *Shah Bano* case was deeply entrenched in the politics of contemporary India. Its fallout marked the beginning of an ugly era of religious fundamentalism in India, with Islamic fundamentalists and right-wing Hindutva[3] groups on either side of the religious divide. And though the case was a watershed in the protection of women's rights in a largely chauvinistic nation, it also showed

---

1   AIR 1985 SC 945.

2   *Shah Bano* has aptly been described as the 'catalyst' for communal conflict in modern India. *See* Anthony Chase, '"Pakistan or the Cemetery!": Muslim Minority Rights in Contemporary India', *Boston College Third World Law Journal*, vol. 16 (1996): p. 35.

3   For an excellent discussion on the emergence of Hindutva in India, *see* Amartya Sen, *The Argumentative Indian*, (New Delhi: Penguin Books India, 2005), p. 49–53.

how the judgements of courts, which are in fact intended to resolve conflicts, can often transform into sources of conflict themselves.[4]

Can a Divorced Muslim Woman Claim Maintenance?

India is a democratic republic founded on the principle that all its citizens are equal. Therefore, there is a common set of laws that binds all citizens, irrespective of religion, race, caste and so forth. However, when it comes to matters involving family affairs—marriage, divorce, maintenance and succession—there are different laws governing people of different faiths. These are known as 'personal laws' and administering them has often led to harsh and unfair results, particularly for women. Consider this in light of the fact that the Constitution embodies an ideal that the state should endeavour to secure a Uniform Civil Code (UCC) across India,[5] to eliminate this very regime of differential governance in family affairs.

In the 1970s and '80s, there were several conflicts surrounding the personal laws governing Muslims alone as against the laws applicable to all Indians. Section 125 of the Code of Criminal Procedure, 1973 (CrPC), which governs all persons, was one such area of conflict. According to this section, a First Class Magistrate could order a husband to provide a monthly allowance of up to 500 rupees[6] to his wife/divorced wife (as

---

4   *See* Yash Ghai, 'Universal Rights and Cultural Pluralism: Universalism and Relativism: Human Rights as a Framework for Negotiating Interethnic Claims', *Yeshiva University Cardozo Law Review*, vol. 21 (2000): p. 1095.

5   Article 44 of the Constitution.

6   The maintenance ceiling of 500 rupees (approximately 11 US dollars, by current exchange rates) per month was eliminated in 2001. However, by virtue of state

long as she had not remarried) if he neglected to maintain her and she was unable to maintain herself.[7] If the husband did not obey the magistrate's order, he could be imprisoned. The law aimed to bring swift relief to the women who were economically dependent on their husbands; it was a 'benign provision enacted to ameliorate the economic condition of neglected wives and discarded divorcees'.[8]

Section 127 of the CrPC provides that if a wife was paid any money on divorce under the personal law governing her, any order for maintenance passed under Section 125 was to be cancelled. The obvious purpose of this was to ensure that if a wife were provided for under personal law, she would not proceed against her husband under the CrPC as well and double-dip. This seems fair enough. Yet, it gave rise to a quandary.

Mahr is a marriage-gift given to the bride in Islam, settled upon before marriage. It may be given either promptly (immediately at the time of marriage) or deferred to a later date. In many cases the payment of mahr is deferred up to when the husband dies or the marriage is dissolved by divorce. The Supreme Court faced a challenge in two cases[9]: Would the payment of mahr, regardless of how insignificant that payment was, absolve a Muslim husband from providing for his divorced wife under Section 125 of the CrPC? In both cases, the court answered in the negative, stating

---

legislation, some states in India have only marginally increased the ceiling instead of eliminating it altogether. For instance, the maintenance ceiling in Maharashtra, Tripura and West Bengal still stands at a paltry 1500 rupees (approximately 33 US dollars) per month.

7　This provision similarly governed the provision of maintenance to children and parents.

8　*Bai Tahira v. Ali Hussain* (AIR 1979 SC 362).

9　Ibid.; *Fuzlunbi v. K. Khader Vali* (AIR 1980 SC 1730).

that the payment of mahr was no bar to granting maintenance. If the mahr amount were insufficient, the court was free to order the payment of maintenance. Though significant, these decisions were relatively inconspicuous and did not receive much coverage in the mainstream media till the *Shah Bano* case emerged.

Facts of the Case

In 1978, a prosperous Muslim lawyer[10] unilaterally divorced Shah Bano, his wife of over forty years by pronouncing 'triple talaq'.[11] The abrupt divorce was allegedly because of an inheritance dispute between Shah Bano's children and those of her husband's other wife.[12]

Now, as mandated by Muslim personal law, the husband paid 3000 rupees (the pre-agreed mahr amount) to his divorced wife during *iddat*.[13] Having been driven out of her matrimonial home in Madhya Pradesh, Shah Bano filed a petition under Section 125 of the CrPC before the Judicial Magistrate at Indore. She sought maintenance from her former husband, who she claimed had an annual professional income of about 60,000 rupees. The magistrate ordered the husband to pay Shah Bano a paltry

---

10 Louise Harmon and Eileen Kaufman, 'Dazzling the World: A Study of India's Constitutional Amendment Mandating Reservations for Women on Rural Panchayats', *Berkeley Women's Law Journal*, vol. 19 (2004): p. 32.

11 'Triple talaq' is an irreversible mode of divorce amongst Sunni Muslims—the husband utters the word 'talaq' thrice, after which the marriage is considered dissolved. India has not banned this form of divorce though many other nations—including Pakistan, Bangladesh, Turkey, Indonesia and Tunisia—prohibit it.

12 Martha Nussbaum, 'India: Implementing Sex Equality Through Law', *Chicago Journal of International Law*, vol. 2 (2001): p. 35.

13 The term refers to the three-month period directly following the divorce, during which a Muslim woman is not permitted to remarry.

twenty-five rupees every month as maintenance. When Shah Bano appealed to the Madhya Pradesh High Court in 1979, the maintenance amount was revised to Rs 179.20 every month. It was then that Shah Bano's former husband, Mohammed Ahmed Khan, petitioned the Supreme Court in 1981 to challenge the high court's decision.

The case could have been a straightforward one. There were already two Supreme Court decisions precisely stating that the court could order a maintenance payment under Section 125 despite the payment of mahr. However, when the matter came up before a two-judge bench of the court the judges were of the opinion that the existing judgements were not robust and had not been correctly decided. Therefore, a five-judge Constitution Bench was formed to resolve the issue. Interestingly, of these five judges, four were Hindu[14] and the fifth, Justice O. Chinnappa Reddy, 'rejected any religious label'.[15]

Mohammed Ahmed Khan argued that according to Muslim law, a husband's liability after divorce extended only up to the iddat period—this would therefore override the general law embodied in the CrPC. Moreover, the order for maintenance under Section 125 was liable to be cancelled under Section 127, since he had tendered the mahr as a payment 'on divorce'.

The Supreme Court eloquently framed the agonizing questions before it in the *Shah Bano* case:

Is the law so ruthless in its inequality that, no matter how much the husband pays for the maintenance of his divorced

14 Chief Justice Y.V. Chandrachud and Justices D.A. Desai, E.S. Venkataramiah and Ranganath Misra.

15 George H. Gadbois, Jr, *Judges of the Supreme Court of India* (New Delhi: Oxford University Press, 2011), p. 351.

wife during the period of iddat, the mere fact that he has paid something, no matter how little, absolves him forever from the duty of paying adequately so as to enable her to keep her body and soul together? Then again, is there any provision in the Muslim Personal Law under which a sum is payable to the wife 'on divorce'?[16]

Maintenance, Mahr and Muslim Law

The Constitution Bench delivered a unanimous verdict. First, the court alluded to the religious neutrality of Section 125 of the CrPC, stating that whether the spouses were 'Hindus or Muslims, Christians or Parsis, pagans or heathens' was 'wholly irrelevant'.[17] Its interpretation was that the underlying purpose of Section 125 was to protect dependents from vagrancy and destitution—thus it saw no reason to exclude Muslims from its sweeping ambit.

Then, the court distinguished between the subject areas covered by Muslim personal law and Section 125 of the CrPC. According to it, Muslim personal law did not address the situation envisaged in Section 125. Yes, the personal law mandated that mahr should be paid during iddat, but it did not contemplate a scenario where the divorced wife was unable to maintain herself after the period of iddat ended. In such a scenario, she would be entitled to seek maintenance under Section 125 of the CrPC. Thus, using deft interpretative tools, the court reconciled Muslim personal law and Section 125. In any event, the court stated that if there was a perceived conflict

16 *Shah Bano* at para. 3.

17 *Shah Bano* at para. 7.

between the two, the CrPC would override the provisions of Muslim personal law.[18]

The court refused to accept the argument that the order for maintenance under Section 125 could be cancelled under Section 127, simply because the husband had made a payment to the wife at the time of divorce, under Muslim personal law. It asserted that mahr was not a payment liable to be made to a Muslim woman 'on divorce'. Exploring the meaning of mahr, the court concluded that it was an amount that a wife was entitled to in *consideration* of marriage—it could not be construed as a divorce payment. The mere fact that mahr was sometimes paid at the time of dissolution of the marriage (by death or by divorce) did not imply that the payment was 'occasioned by' the divorce. By thus defining mahr as a marriage payment, rather than a divorce payment, the court emphasized that the payment of mahr could not bar courts from also awarding maintenance.

To support the view that awarding maintenance would not go against the tenets of Islam, the bench also interpreted sections of the Quran to mean that husbands were duty-bound to maintain their wives.

The court confirmed the maintenance amount awarded by the Madhya Pradesh High Court (Rs 179.20 every month), and also awarded to Shah Bano the legal costs of the appeal, which it fixed at 10,000 rupees.

---

18 The court's rationale was that although Muslim men were allowed to have up to four wives, Section 125 of the CrPC also recognized that a wife (irrespective of religion) had the right to stay away from her husband and seek maintenance from him if he had another wife. Since no exception for Muslims (who would otherwise be permitted to have up to four wives) was carved out of this provision, the court in *Shah Bano* inferred that Section 125 would prevail over Muslim personal law.

The operative part of the judgement was followed by deep dissatisfaction over the legislature's failure to establish a UCC for all citizens, in accordance with Article 44 of the Constitution. It expressed anguish that Article 44 had remained a dead letter and stated that concrete steps were needed if the Constitution of India was to 'have any meaning'.[19] The court seemed to have used the absence of a UCC to justify its interventionist approach in an issue of religious policy:

> The role of the reformer has to be assumed by the courts because it is beyond the endurance of sensitive minds to allow injustice to be suffered when it is so palpable. But piecemeal attempts of courts to bridge the gap between personal laws cannot take the place of a common Civil Code.[20]

These aspects of the Supreme Court's judgement were relatively non-controversial. It was not the decision itself, but the manner in which it was taken, that provoked public controversy. This is precisely why, although two Supreme Court judgements had largely already said what was said in the *Shah Bano* case, the latter was the cynosure of widespread attention from the media and civil society.

The *Shah Bano* judgement was laced with undertones suggesting that the court was critical of Muslim personal law, especially in the context of its treatment of women. For instance, the court stated that a Muslim husband enjoys the privilege of being able to discard his wife whenever he chose to do so, 'for

---

19 *Shah Bano* at para. 35.
20 Ibid.

reasons good, bad or indifferent. Indeed, for no reason at all'.[21] The court added that the Prophet was ascribed the statement, 'hopefully wrongly', that a woman was made from a crooked rib, and if you tried to bend it straight, it would break—therefore treat your wives kindly.[22]

After the Judgement, the Juggernaut of Reactions and an Anticlimax

There was sensational press coverage, vociferous protests and counter-protests by members of civil society, and immense indignation among many Muslim theologians as a result of the Supreme Court's observations in the *Shah Bano* case. The main repercussion of the judgement was the opening up of a deep divide not only between Hindus and Muslims, but also among different sections of Muslims.[23] Conservative Muslims opposed the judgement while liberal Muslims, Hindus and advocates of feminism backed it. The agitation of the conservative Muslims, though, received greater visibility and had a wider impact than protests by liberal Muslims.

What caused the outrage amongst conservative Muslims? A combination of factors. Several Muslims were upset that five non-Muslim judges, with backgrounds in secular law, took it upon themselves to interpret sections of the Quran—a challenge even to scholars of Muslim law.[24] Muslim clergymen believed

---

21 *Shah Bano* at para. 3.

22 Ibid., para. 1.

23 *See* Henry Steiner and Philip Alston, *International Human Rights in Context* (Oxford: Oxford University Press, 2000), p. 508.

24 *See* Shalina A. Chibber, 'Charting a New Path Toward Gender Equality in India: From Religious Personal Laws to a Uniform Civil Code', *Indiana Law Journal*, vol.

that it was most inappropriate for a secular court to interpret religious law and that it would set a bad precedent.[25] That the bench relied on western interpretations of the Quran did not help the judgement gain legitimacy.

There was a strong perception that the *Shah Bano* decision, rather than being a simple maintenance award, was unduly critical of Muslim law and Islamic practices.[26] The court's contemptuous tone and uncharitable comments (such as the 'crooked rib' remark) did not go down well with Muslim conservatives. They were apprehensive that the judgement would compromise their identity and autonomy. They were suspicious that it was a step towards assimilating them into mainstream Hindu culture.[27] They questioned the state's commitment to the values of pluralism and heterodoxy.

Perhaps the most logical criticism of the judgement on secular grounds is the fact that the court could have decided in Shah Bano's favour based on constitutional principles, without interpreting Muslim law (which was done in two cases

---

83 (2008): p. 695; Seval Yildirim, 'Expanding Secularism's Scope: An Indian Case Study', *The American Journal of Comparative Law*, vol. 52 (2004): p. 901.

25 *See* Robert D. Baird, 'Traditional Values, Governmental Values, and Religious Conflict in Contemporary India', *Brigham Young University Law Review*, vol. 1998 (1998): p. 337; Srikanth Reddy, 'What Would Your Founding Fathers Think? What India's Constitution Says—And What Its Framers Would Say—About the Current Debate Over a Uniform Civil Code', *George Washington International Law Review*, vol. 41 (2009): p. 405.

26 Josh Goodman, 'Divine Judgement: Judicial Review of Religious Legal Systems in India and Israel', *Hastings International and Comparative Law Review*, vol. 32 (2009): p. 477.

27 Mark Calaguas, Cristina Drost and Edward Fluet, 'Legal Pluralism and Women's Rights: A Study in Postcolonial Tanzania', *Columbia Journal of Gender and Law*, vol. 16 (2007): p. 471.

before *Shah Bano*).[28] The court ventured into hazardous territory when it invoked its own interpretation of the Quran.

The court's appeal to enact a UCC in the *Shah Bano* judgement was counterproductive. Until the judgement, Muslims were willing to consider the idea of a uniform set of laws governing family affairs. However, the *Shah Bano* decision introduced scepticism amongst some Muslims that a UCC would mean a majoritarian code of rules.[29]

And yet, it is very unfair to criticize the peripheral elements of the court's judgement without acknowledging the values of gender equality, and the protection and independence of women that the court espoused in the crux of its judgement. Several people saw the judgement as a vindication of the rights of women in Islamic law. *Shah Bano* constitutes one of the few accolades earned by the highest court of the land—which has historically been perceived as a male-dominated court—in the area of women's rights.

The scathing reactions of a large segment of Muslims led to an anticlimax; a total volte-face. Having come under tremendous pressure from her community, Shah Bano affixed her thumbprint on a letter retracting her involvement with the cause—a fight that persisted over seven years and took her everywhere, from the Court of the Judicial Magistrate to the Supreme Court. She dissociated herself from the Supreme Court judgement,[30]

---

28 *See* Cyra Akila Choudhury, '(Mis)appropriated Liberty: Identity, Gender Justice, and Muslim Personal Law Reform in India', *Columbia Journal of Gender and Law*, vol. 17 (2008): p. 45; Sara Ahmad, 'Judicial Complicity with Communal Violence in India', *Northwestern Journal of International Law and Business*, vol. 17 (1996): p. 320.

29 *See* Chibber, 'Charting a New Path Toward Gender Equality in India', p. 695.

30 Steiner and Alston, *International Human Rights in Context*, p. 508.

allegedly because she was 'explained' that her salvation would depend upon whether she sought maintenance or not.[31]

The Overruling: Vote-Bank Politics at Its Worst

The protests and counter-protests over the *Shah Bano* judgement persisted. Initially, the Rajiv Gandhi-led Congress Party which had won the parliamentary elections of 1984 by a sweeping majority, favoured the judgement.[32] However, after suffering losses in state elections in some Muslim-dominated regions, the government changed its approach. It succumbed to vote-bank politics. There were calls among Muslim conservatives asking for the Parliament to pass a law nullifying the Supreme Court judgement in the *Shah Bano* case. Despite a spirited defence of the judgement in Parliament by Muslim leader Arif Mohammed Khan,[33] the Rajiv Gandhi government crumbled under pressure and enacted the Muslim Women (Protection of Rights in Divorce) Act, 1986 (the MWA).[34]

Contrary to its name, the MWA actually undermined the far-reaching protection granted to divorced Muslim women in *Shah Bano* and other similar judgements. It was more in the nature of a 'dissolution of rights in divorce' act rather than a 'protection of rights in divorce' act. According to the MWA, mahr and maintenance were to be paid to a divorced Muslim woman only during the three-month iddat. It effectively deprived

---

31 Nussbaum, 'India: Implementing Sex Equality Through Law', p. 35.

32 Reddy, 'What Would Your Founding Fathers Think?', p. 405.

33 Bipin Chandra, Mridula Mukherjee, and Aditya Mukherjee, *India after Independence* (New Delhi: Penguin Books, 2000), p. 285.

34 *See* Appendix on p. 67 for the full text of the MWA.

Muslim women of the right to file a maintenance petition under Section 125 of the CrPC.[35] What divorced women who were financially dependent on their husbands were expected to do after the expiry of iddat was anyone's guess.

Muslim as well as Hindu supporters of the *Shah Bano* decision were miffed at the haste with which the MWA was enacted. Muslim women were infuriated that the government of the day treated the opinion of one segment of conservative Muslims as representative of all Muslims. Shahjahan, a Muslim feminist, famously protested in front of the Parliament in New Delhi, stating that if Muslim women were not treated like citizens of India (because of the enactment of separate laws for them), they should be allowed to form another country called Auratstan (literally 'the land of women').[36] Right-wing Hindus, on the other hand, were distressed because Muslims were getting preferential treatment.

The legislative overruling of the *Shah Bano* decision was the start of an ugly brand of vote-bank politics in India. The right-wing Bharatiya Janata Party (BJP) capitalized on the dissent against the Congress government amongst Hindus. From holding two parliamentary seats in 1984, the BJP cashed in on its Hindutva movement, winning eighty-five seats in 1989, 119 seats in 1991, and finally, 182 seats in 1998, to become the single largest party in the National Democratic Alliance (NDA). It remained the NDA's single largest party and governed India until its defeat in the parliamentary elections of 2004.

---

35 Madhavi Sunder, 'Piercing the Veil', *Yale Law Journal*, vol. 112 (2003): p. 1399.

36 Vrinda Narain, 'Negotiating the Boundaries: Gender and Community in India' (LLM thesis, Faculty of Graduate Studies and Research, McGill University, Montreal (1997)), http://digitool.library.mcgill.ca/webclient/StreamGate?folder_id=0&dvs=1314105126817-658 (accessed 10 January 2013).

The *Shah Bano* judgement was also one of the catalysts of a violent right-wing Hindutva movement that spread across the country. Right-wing Hindu extremism plummeted to its lowest point in 1992, when the Babri Masjid in Ayodhya was destroyed in a high-handed act of Hindu fundamentalism. The Sangh Parivar,[37] which was allegedly responsible for the atrocity, claimed that the site of the mosque was the birthplace of Lord Rama, and that a few centuries ago the original temple at the site had been destroyed/modified to create the mosque. This unilateral act of historical retribution sparked off communal riots in several Indian cities, particularly in Mumbai (then Bombay). The riots culminated in a series of thirteen coordinated bomb blasts in Bombay on 12 March 1993, which claimed over 250 lives.[38] It is hardly surprising that many believe that the enactment of the MWA was the initial fuel for the demolition of the Babri Masjid and the communal violence that flared up as a result.[39]

The *Danial Latifi* Case and What Followed

In 1994, a few years after it was enacted, there was an unsuccessful constitutional challenge to the MWA in the Supreme Court.[40] A writ petition was filed under Article 32 of the Constitution, invoking the Supreme Court to declare the MWA as void and arbitrary, and also to consider enacting a UCC for all citizens of India. The Supreme Court dismissed the petition, stating

---

37 A right-wing consortium of Hindu organizations; the BJP is the primary political arm of the Sangh Parivar.

38 *See* Thomas Hansen, *Wages of Violence: Naming and Identity in Postcolonial Bombay* (New Jersey: Princeton University Press, 2001), p. 125.

39 Goodman, 'Divine Judgement: Judicial Review of Religious Legal Systems', p. 477.

40 *Maharshi Avadhesh v. Union of India* (1994 Supp (1) SCC 713).

that such matters were within the domain of the legislature, not the judiciary.

Meanwhile, several high courts began interpreting the MWA to endorse the proposition that divorced Muslim women be entitled to maintenance not only during the three-month iddat, but also after that.[41] They asserted that the MWA only specified that the mahr amount had to be paid as a lump sum to the divorced wife during iddat; the amount, however, should be sufficient for the wife's future maintenance. Other high courts concluded that the husband's liability under the MWA was limited to the period of iddat, after which the divorced wife (if she could not maintain herself) would have to approach her relatives or the Muslim Wakf Board for maintenance.[42]

The Supreme Court ended this divergence of opinions in *Danial Latifi v. Union of India*[43] (*Danial Latifi*). Danial Latifi, a senior advocate and an authority on Islamic law, who had in fact represented Shah Bano in the Supreme Court, challenged the constitutional validity of the MWA.[44] He argued that the MWA

---

41 *Arab Ahemadhia Abdulla v. Arab Bail Mohmuna* (AIR 1988 Guj 141) (Gujarat High Court); *Ali v. Sufaira* ((1988) 3 Crimes 147) (Kerala High Court); *K. Kunhashed Hazi v. Amena* (1995 Cr.L.J 3371) (Kerala High Court); *K. Zunaideen v. Ameena Begum* ((1998) II DMC 468)(Madras High Court); *Karim Abdul Shaik v. Shenaz Karim Shaik* (2000 Cr.L.J. 3560) (Bombay High Court); *Jaitunbi Mubarak Shaikh v. Mubarak Fakruddin Shaikh* (1999 (3) Mh LJ 694) (Bombay High Court); *Kaka v. Hassan Bano* (II (1998) DMC 85) (Punjab and Haryana High Court).

42 *Usman Khan v. Fathimnurisa* (AIR 1990 AP 225) (Andhra Pradesh High Court); *Abdul Rashid v. Sultana Begum* (1992 Cr.L.J. 76) (Calcutta High Court); *Abdul Haq v. Yasima Talat* (1998 Cr.L.J. 3433) (Madhya Pradesh High Court); *Md. Marahim v. Raiza Begum* (1993 (1) DMC 60) (Madras High Court).

43 (2001) 7 SCC 740.

44 This petition was clubbed and decided along with several other petitions that also challenged the constitutionality of the MWA. Despite the unsuccessful challenge of the MWA before the Supreme Court a few years earlier, these petitions were admitted and referred to a five-judge Constitution Bench.

contravened the right to equality (Articles 14 and 15) as well as the right to life (Article 21) guaranteed by the Constitution. Rejecting this challenge, the court emphasized that the MWA ensured that a husband would not only maintain his divorced wife during iddat, but also pay a lump sum that would amount to a reasonable and fair provision for her future. Although the Supreme Court went against the obvious legislative intent behind the enactment of the MWA, it interpreted the law so as to truly protect Muslim women. Divorced Muslim women could now seek a lump sum settlement from their former husbands under the MWA, which would serve as their maintenance during iddat as well as provide for their future.

In *Danial Latifi*, the Supreme Court exercised greater restraint than in *Shah Bano*. It refused to strike down the MWA, yet protected the rights of divorced Muslim women through an astute use of interpretative tools. Keenly aware of the repercussions of the *Shah Bano* judgement, the court handled the case with 'restraint and diplomacy'.[45]

In another case,[46] the Supreme Court said that even if a divorced Muslim woman (who had not remarried) filed a petition under Section 125 of the CrPC, the petition would not be dismissed on the technicality of failing to make a claim under the MWA. The conjoint effect of two recent decisions of the Supreme Court[47] is that a divorced Muslim woman is free

45 *See* Goodman, 'Divine Judgement: Judicial Review of Religious Legal Systems', p. 477.

46 *Iqbal Bano v. State of Uttar Pradesh* (AIR 2007 SC 2215).

47 *Shabana Bano v. Imran Khan* (AIR 2010 SC 305); *Iqbal Bano v. State of Uttar Pradesh* (AIR 2007 SC 2215).

to either seek maintenance under Section 125 of the CrPC or claim lump sum alimony under the MWA.[48]

Two and a half decades after the *Shah Bano* case, which gave relief to divorced Muslim women, and the MWA, which deprived them of that relief, Indian courts have unshackled and expanded the rights of divorced Muslim women. Now, a divorced Muslim woman can file a petition either under the CrPC (for recurring maintenance) or through the MWA (for lump sum settlement), seeking fair and reasonable provision for the rest of her life.

Feminism v. Secularism

Although mired in controversy, the *Shah Bano* judgement can arguably be considered as the 'greatest contribution' to the development of Muslim law.[49] However, its aftermath revealed some harsh realities about what happens when women's rights and religious tenets collide in a democracy. The hurried codification and enactment of the MWA proved that gender equality would succumb to the realities of pluralism.[50] Feminism will languish low in the priority list of governments when it is pitted against a large vote share.

---

48 *See* Flavia Agnes, 'Shah Bano to Shabana Bano', *Indian Express*, 15 December 2009, http://www.indianexpress.com/news/shah-bano-to-shabana-bano/554314/ (accessed 28 November 2012).

49 Danial Latifi, 'Muslim Law' in *Fifty Years of the Supreme Court of India: Its Grasp and Reach*, eds S.K. Verma and Kusum Kumar (New Delhi: Oxford University Press, 2003), p. 275.

50 Radhika Coomaraswamy, 'Reinventing International Law: Women's Rights as Human Rights in the International Community' (The Edward A. Smith Lecture, Human Rights Program, Harvard Law School, 1997).

Indeed, the *Shah Bano* judgement uncovered conflicts at intricate levels—between the emancipation of women and their belonging to a minority community, between safeguarding religious traditions and ushering in a democracy that applies a uniform set of civil laws to all citizens regardless of religious affiliations, and between lawmakers and courts (on who would have the last word in areas where law and religion overlapped).

The bright side is that the law of the land today gives two meaningful remedies to protect divorced Muslim women from poverty and destitution. But the journey to this position has been an arduous one. From right-wing Hindutva politics to appeasing minorities, from defiled places of worship to communal riots, much water has passed under the bridge.

Although Shah Bano didn't eventually claim her alimony from her former husband, there are many divorced Muslim women who will. It can only be hoped that the next Shah Bano case is met with responses rather than reactions by the political class.

APPENDIX

The Muslim Women (Protection of Rights on Divorce) Act, 1986

An Act to protect the right of Muslim women who have been divorced by, or have obtained divorce from, their husbands, and to provide for matters connected therewith or incidental thereto.

BE it enacted by Parliament in the thirty-seventh year of the Republic of India as follows:

1. Short title and extent
1) This Act may be called the Muslim Women (Protection of Rights on Divorce) Act, 1986.
2) It extends to the whole of India except the State of Jammu and Kashmir.

2. Definitions
In this Act, unless the context otherwise requires:
a) "divorced woman" means a Muslim woman who was married according to Muslim law, and has been divorced by, or has obtained divorce from her husband in accordance with Muslim law;
b) "iddat period" means, in the case of a divorced woman:
   i) three menstrual courses after the date of divorce, if she is subject to menstruation;
   ii) three lunar months after her divorce, if she is not subject to menstruation; and
   iii) if she is enceinte at the time of her divorce, the period

between the divorce and the delivery of her child or the termination of her pregnancy, whichever is earlier;

c) "Magistrate" means a Magistrate of the First Class exercising jurisdiction under the Code of Criminal Procedure, 1973 in the area where the divorced woman resides;

d) "prescribed" means prescribed by rules made under this Act.

3. Mahr or other properties of Muslim woman to be given to her at the time of divorce:

1) Notwithstanding anything contained in any other law for the time being in force, a divorced woman shall be entitled to:

a) a reasonable and fair provision and maintenance to be made and paid to her within the iddat period by her former husband;

b) where she herself maintains the children born to her before or after the divorce, a reasonable and fair provision and maintenance to be made and paid by her former husband for a period of two years from the respective dates of birth of such children;

c) an amount equal to the sum of mahr or dower agreed to be paid to her at the time or her marriage or at any time thereafter according to Muslim Law; and

d) all the properties given to her before or at the time or marriage or after her marriage by her relatives or friends or the husband or any relatives of the husband or his friends.

2) Where a reasonable and fair provision and maintenance or the amount of mahr or dower due has not been made or paid or the properties referred to in clause (d) of sub-

section (1) have not been delivered to a divorced woman on her divorce, she or any one duly authorized by her may, on her behalf, make an application to a Magistrate for an order for payment of such provision and maintenance, mahr or dower or the delivery of properties, as the case may be.

3) Where an application has been made under sub-section (2) by a divorced woman, the Magistrate may, if he is satisfied that:

   a) her husband having sufficient means, has failed or neglected to make or pay her within the iddat period a reasonable and fair provision and maintenance for her and the children; or

   b) the amount equal to the sum of mahr or dower has not been paid or that the properties referred to in clause (d) of sub-section (1) have not been paid or that the properties referred to in clause (d) of sub-section (1) have not been delivered to her, make an order, within one month of the date of the filing of the application, directing her former husband to pay such reasonable and fair provision and maintenance to the divorced woman as he may determine as fit and proper having regard to the needs of the divorced woman, the standard of life enjoyed by her during her marriage and the means of her former husband or, as the case may be, for the payment of such mahr or dower or the delivery of such properties referred to in clause (d) of sub-section (1) to the divorced woman:

   Provided that if the Magistrate finds it impracticable to dispose of the application within the said period, he may, for reasons to be recorded by him, dispose of the application after the said period.

4) If any person against whom an order has been made under sub-section (3) fails without sufficient cause to comply with the order, the Magistrate may issue a warrant for levying the amount of maintenance or mahr or dower due in the manner provided for levying fines under the Code of Criminal Procedure, 1973, and may sentence such person, for the whole or part of any amount remaining unpaid after the execution of the warrant, to imprisonment for a term which may extend to one year or until payment if sooner made, subject to such person being heard in defence and the said sentence being imposed according to the provisions of the said Code.

4. Order for payment of maintenance

1) Notwithstanding anything contained in the foregoing provisions of this Act or in any other law for the time being in force, where a Magistrate is satisfied that a divorced woman has not remarried and is not able to maintain herself after the iddat period, he may make an order directing such of her relatives as would be entitled to inherit her property on her death according to Muslim law to pay such reasonable and fair maintenance to her as he may determine fit and proper, having regard to the needs of the divorced woman, the standard of life enjoyed by her during her marriage and the means of such relatives, and such maintenance shall be payable by such relatives in the proportions in which they would inherit her property and at such periods as he may specify in his order:

Provided that where such divorced woman has children, the Magistrate shall order only such children to pay maintenance to her, and in the event of any such children being unable to pay such maintenance, the Magistrate shall order the parents of such divorced woman to pay maintenance to her:

Provided further that if any of the parents is unable to pay his or her share of the maintenance ordered by the Magistrate on the ground of his or her not having the means to pay the same, the Magistrate may, on proof of such inability being furnished to him, order that the share of such relatives in the maintenance ordered by him be paid by such of the other relatives as may appear to the Magistrate to have the means of paying the same in such proportions as the Magistrate may think fit to order.

2) Where a divorced woman is unable to maintain herself and she has no relatives as mentioned in sub-section (1) or such relatives or any one of them have not enough means to pay the maintenance ordered the Magistrate or the other relatives have not the means to pay the shares of those relatives whose shares have been ordered by the Magistrate to be paid by such other relatives under the second proviso to sub-section (1), the Magistrate may, by order, direct the State Wakf Board established under Section 9 of the Wakf Act, 1954, or under any other law for the time being in force in a state, functioning in the area in which the woman resides, to pay such maintenance as determined by him under sub-section (1) or, as the case may be, to pay the shares of such of the relatives who are unable to pay, at such periods as he may specify in his order.

5. **Opinion to be governed by the provisions of Sections 125
    to 128 of Act 2 of 1974**

    If, on the date of the first hearing of the application under
    sub-section (2) of Section 3, a divorced woman and her
    former husband declare, by affidavit or any other declaration
    in writing in such form as may be prescribed, either jointly
    or separately, that they would prefer to be governed by the
    provisions of Sections 125 to 128 of the Code of Criminal
    Procedure, 1973, and file such affidavit or declaration in the
    Court hearing the application, the Magistrate shall dispose
    of such application accordingly.

    Explanation: For the purposes of this section, "date of the
    first hearing of the application" means the date fixed in
    the summons for the attendance of the respondent to the
    application.

6. **Power to make rules**

1) The Central Government may, by notification in the Official
    Gazette, make rules for carrying out the purposes of this Act.

2) In particular and without prejudice to the foregoing power,
    such rules may provide for:

    a) The form of the affidavit or other declaration in
        writing to be filed under Section 5;

    b) The procedure to be followed by the Magistrate in
        disposing of applications under this Act, including the
        serving of notices to the parties to such applications,
        dates of hearing of such applications and other matters;

    c) Any other matter which is required to be or may be
        prescribed.

3) Every rule made under this Act shall be laid, as soon as may be after it is made, before each House of Parliament, while it is in session, for a total period of thirty days which may be comprised in one session or in two or more successive sessions, and if, before the expiry of the session immediately following the session or the successive sessions aforesaid, both Houses agree in making any modification in the rule or both Houses agree that the rule should not be made, the rule shall thereafter have effect only in such modified form or be of no effect, as the case may be; so however, that any such modification or annulment shall be without prejudice to the validity of anything previously done under that rule.

7. Transitional provisions

Every application by a divorced woman under Section 125 or under Section 127 of the Code of Criminal Procedure, 1973 pending before a Magistrate on the commencement of this Act, shall, notwithstanding anything contained in that Code and subjected to the provisions of Section 5 of this Act, be disposed of by such Magistrate in accordance with the provisions of this Act.

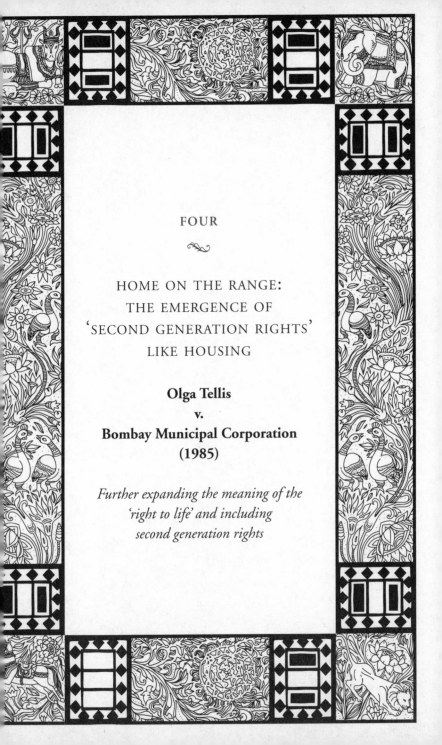

FOUR

HOME ON THE RANGE:
THE EMERGENCE OF
'SECOND GENERATION RIGHTS'
LIKE HOUSING

Olga Tellis
v.
Bombay Municipal Corporation
(1985)

Further expanding the meaning of the
'right to life' and including
second generation rights

CONVENTIONALLY, HUMAN RIGHTS have been divided into two broad categories: civil and political or 'first generation rights'—including the right to life, the right against arbitrary arrest and detention, and the right to freedom—and social, economic and cultural rights or 'second generation rights', such as the right to health and the right to social security. Like most other Constitutions from which it drew inspiration, the Constitution of India was framed such that only first generation rights were fundamental rights which could be enforced by courts of law; on the other hand, several second generation rights[1] were encompassed as non-binding aspirations in the nature of directive principles of state policy.

In the early years after Independence, Indian courts unwaveringly followed this framework of rights conceptualized by the Constituent Assembly and were generally willing only to enforce first generation rights. Then, in the 1970s and '80s, an interesting phenomenon came about—due to strong judicial activism, the courts expanded the scope of several fundamental rights, particularly Article 21 of the Constitution,[2]

---

1 For instance, equal pay for equal work and raising the level of nutrition and standard of living of the people.

2 Article 21 of the Constitution reads: 'No person shall be deprived of his life or personal liberty except according to procedure established by law.'

to include second generation rights within their ambit.[3]

Contextually, *Olga Tellis v. Bombay Municipal Corporation*[4] (*Olga Tellis*) was one of the pioneering cases through which the Supreme Court brought socio-economic rights within the sweep of Part III of the Constitution (encompassing fundamental rights)—holding that the right to shelter was a fundamental right and thus impacting millions of slum/pavement dwellers in India. It reflected the gradual transition of the Supreme Court from merely recognizing fundamental rights, which are framed negatively as negative obligations (in the nature of commands preventing the state from acting in a certain manner), to elevating them to the level of positive duties to be performed by the state. By including the right to shelter within its reach, the Supreme Court attributed a new socio-economic dimension to Article 21.[5] And that is why *Olga Tellis* was a milestone in the recognition of second generation human rights by Indian courts.

Facts of the Case

Every year, lakhs of people from rural areas flock to Mumbai in search of work. Slum/pavement dwellers in Mumbai, like migrants in any urban area, generally reside in the areas that are nearest to their place of work or business. In July 1981, the then chief minister of Maharashtra, A.R. Antulay, publicly announced that all residents of Mumbai (then Bombay) who

---

3   Jayna Kothari, 'A Right to Housing?', *India Together*, April 2002, www.indiatogether. org/opinions/rhousing02.htm (accessed 28 November 2012).

4   AIR 1986 SC 180.

5   Vijayashri Sripati, 'Toward Fifty Years of Constitutionalism and Fundamental Rights in India: Looking Back to See Ahead', *American University International Law Review*, vol. 14 (1998): p. 413.

were living in informal settlements or squatting on pavements of major roads, but did not possess photo-passes would be forcibly evicted, and either deported to their respective places of origin or transported to places outside Mumbai. Antulay also directed the Commissioner of Police to assist the Bombay Municipal Corporation (the BMC) in carrying out this mass eviction and demolition drive. The apparent justification that the chief minister offered for his announcement was: 'It [the life of slum/ pavement dwellers in Mumbai] is a very inhuman existence. These structures are flimsy and open to the elements. During the monsoon, there is no way these people can live comfortably.'[6]

The Municipal Commissioner of Bombay went ahead and ordered the removal of these 'encroachments' under Sections 312–14 of the Mumbai Municipal Corporation Act, 1888 (the BMC Act). Section 314 authorized the municipal commissioner to remove encroachments without prior notice. At the time, this legislation was nearly a century old and it still stands as the constituent instrument of the Municipal Corporation of Greater Mumbai. In response, two groups of slum/pavement dwellers residing in Mumbai filed writ petitions before the Supreme Court of India, challenging the constitutional validity of Sections 312–14 of the BMC Act.

Interestingly, the petitioners in *Olga Tellis* did not contend that they were entitled to live on pavements. They contended instead that they had a right to life and personal liberty under Article 21 of the Constitution, and that right necessarily included the right to livelihood. Given that slum/pavement dwellers had migrated to the city from rural areas to find means of basic

---

6 *Olga Tellis* at para. 5.

sustenance, living on pavements as close to their workplace as possible was vital to their survival. They contended that their right to life was illusory without the right to protection (by the state) of the means by which such a life could be lived.[7] Simply put, the petitioners argued that the law cannot provide you with something but deprive you of something else without which the former itself is meaningless. For instance, the right to own a vehicle has little value unless there is a corresponding right to buy fuel to run the vehicle.

As a remedy for being evicted from their homes, the petitioners claimed alternative accommodation. They also asserted that it is impermissible to classify pavement dwellers as trespassers, since they occupied pavements not by choice, but due to economic compulsions. The situation was one of dire necessity, and it compelled them to use public property for personal survival.[8]

On the other hand, the BMC stated that Sections 312–14 of the BMC Act were conceived in public interest and 'great care was taken to ensure that no harassment is caused to pavement dwellers by evicting them'. An oxymoronic argument! What can be a greater act of harassment to pavement dwellers than evicting them from their homes? The BMC also cited significant hazards to health and safety, including an increase in crime rates and environmental degradation, as its grounds for evicting the petitioners. It claimed that the occupation of public pavements augments the spread of contagious diseases, and that the presence of pavement dwellers increases the risk of traffic accidents, as pedestrians have nowhere but the streets to walk on.

---

7   *Olga Tellis* at para. 62.

8   Ibid., paragraphs 62 and 73.

The challenge before the Supreme Court was to reconcile the right to life of the pavement dwellers with the right to health and safety of the community at large.

The Right to Life Includes the Right to Livelihood

The most striking aspect of the Supreme Court's judgement was the candid manner in which it analysed the case, maintaining a clear focus on the ground realities without reference to the cryptic. This is tangible in the words with which it opened its judgement:

> Those who have made pavements their homes exist in the midst of filth and squalor, which has to be seen to be believed. Rabid dogs in search of stinking meat and cats in search of hungry rats keep them company. They cook and sleep where they ease, for no conveniences are available to them. Their daughters, come of age, bathe under the nosy gaze of passers-by, unmindful of the feminine sense of bashfulness. The cooking and washing over, women pick lice from each other's hair. The boys beg. Menfolk, without occupation, snatch chains with the connivance of the defenders of law and order; when caught, if at all, they say: 'Who doesn't commit crimes in this city?'[9]

From the perspective of human rights jurisprudence, the observations that the Supreme Court made in its judgement were far more significant than the decision itself. For the first time in its history of thirty-five years, the Supreme Court affirmed that the

---

9   *Olga Tellis* at para. 1.

right to life includes the (second generation) right to livelihood. It reasoned that '[i]f the right to livelihood is not treated as a part of the constitutional right to life, the easiest way of depriving a person his right to life would be to deprive him [or her] of his [or her] means of livelihood to the point of abrogation'.[10] The Supreme Court concluded that slum/pavement dwellers could not be evicted without any loss of their livelihood.[11] It rightly recognized that the right to life is ineffectual without the means by which that right can be meaningfully exercised. Any deprivation of the right to livelihood would have to be in accordance with a procedure established by law that is fair, just and reasonable.[12] However, the court stated, the procedure prescribed by Section 314 of the BMC Act could not be regarded as unfair, unjust or unreasonable. The court's rationale was that Section 314 of the BMC Act conferred discretion on the municipal commissioner to evict unauthorized encroachments, but did not impose a positive mandate on him to do so. This discretion would have to be exercised in a reasonable manner, guided by constitutional principles. Refusing to invalidate the provisions of the BMC Act, the court held in favour of the BMC, and permitted the eviction drive. It opined that no person had the right to encroach upon land that had been earmarked for a public purpose, such as a garden, playground or street.

---

10 *Olga Tellis* at para. 32.

11 H.M. Seervai, *Constitutional Law of India*, 4th ed. (New Delhi: Universal Book Traders, 1999), p. 1185.

12 Article 21 of the Constitution mandates that no person is to be deprived of his right to life and personal liberty except by a procedure established by law. In *Maneka Gandhi v. Union of India* (AIR 1978 SC 597), discussed in Chapter Two, the Supreme Court held that any such procedure established by law must be fair, just and reasonable.

Although the Supreme Court decided in favour of the BMC, it arrived at its decision on the basis of several assurances made by the statutory body, including providing alternative accommodation, implementing socio-economic policies and schemes for rehabilitation, and implementing positive measures to provide equal treatment to the neglected sections of society. The court also held that in no event were slums to be removed until one month after the end of the monsoon season at the time. (This was to ensure that the pavement dwellers would not be stranded during the monsoon, as had indeed been the case in July 1981 soon after Antulay made the initial public announcement.)

Policy-Oriented Approach of the Supreme Court

The Supreme Court's approach reflected its evolving role in the democratic governance of the nation. Although it generally desists from interfering in matters of government policy, *Olga Tellis* was among the first instances when the Supreme Court, under the guise of enforcing a fundamental right, did precisely that. Yet, while the remedies granted by the court were described as unorthodox and while their efficacy was questioned, they have been largely accepted as legitimate.[13] Interestingly, *Olga Tellis* formed one of what eventually became an array of decisions, wherein the court refused to grant any immediate relief to litigants but directed the state to ensure proactive implementation of policies for the protection of the destitute and neglected sections of society. Rather than providing specific

13 *See* Jessie M. Hohmann, 'Visions of Social Transformation and the Invocation of Human Rights in Mumbai: The Struggle for the Right to Housing', *Yale Human Rights & Development Law Journal*, vol. 13(1) (2010): p. 135.

relief to the parties before it, the Supreme Court focused on the broader institutional and policy issues at hand. *Olga Tellis* offers a paradigm example of how the Indian judiciary has elicited political dialogue on issues that would otherwise remain hidden from public scrutiny.[14]

The Aftermath of *Olga Tellis*

Within a few years, *Olga Tellis* received widespread publicity and recognition across the world, particularly in developing countries that faced similar challenges involving urban migration. Though the Supreme Court had authorized eviction, it had not legitimized 'dishousing'.[15] The real victory in *Olga Tellis* lay in the undertakings given by the BMC—the undertakings that signified the state's acceptance of the fact that slum dwellers were indeed entitled to alternative accommodation. In 1990, the Law Commission of India recognized that although statutory law did not provide adequate protection to slum/pavement dwellers, the court had adopted a humane approach in affording them reasonable protection.[16]

Throughout the 1990s, courts in India predominantly upheld the principles laid down in *Olga Tellis*, asserting that the state is constitutionally obliged to provide housing to the weaker and economically disadvantaged segments of society. Numerous

---

14 *See* Craig Scott and Patrick Macklem, 'Constitutional Ropes of Sand or Justiciable Guarantees? Social Rights in a New South African Constitution', *University of Pennsylvania Law Review*, vol. 141 (1992): p. 1.

15 'Dishousing' refers to the deprivation of a person of his/her house or home.

16 *See* Law Commission of India, '138th Report on Legislative Protection for Slum and Pavement Dwellers', 1990, p. 14, www.lawcommissionofindia.nic.in/101-169/Report138.pdf (accessed 29 January 2013).

decisions referred to the right to shelter as expounded in international treaties such as the Universal Declaration of Human Rights (1948) and the International Covenant on Economic, Social and Cultural Rights (1966), and held that this right falls within the ambit of Articles 19[17] and 21 of the Constitution.[18]

In *Ahmedabad Municipal Corporation v. Nawab Khan Gulab Khan*,[19] the pavement dwellers of Rakhial Road, Ahmedabad, filed a writ petition when the city's municipal corporation sought to remove their huts, which had been constructed on footpaths adjoining a main road. In an interim order, the Supreme Court requested the Ahmedabad Municipal Corporation to formulate a scheme to provide alternative accommodation to the pavement dwellers. The court's judgement reiterated the principles laid down in *Olga Tellis* and affirmed that the 'encroachers' were to be given an opportunity to opt for one of a few available schemes for their rehabilitation.

Shantistar Builders v. Narayan Totame[20] was a case concerning the allotment of flats to the weaker sections of society. The Supreme Court went a step further by emphasizing the significance of a minimum standard of accommodation, which is interlinked with a certain quality of life:

The difference between the need of an animal and [that of] a human being for shelter has to be kept in view. For the animal,

---

17 Article 19 of the Constitution comprises the six (originally seven) freedoms granted to the citizens, including the freedom of speech and expression and the freedom to assemble peaceably without arms.

18 *See* Kothari, 'A Right to Housing?', www.indiatogether.org/opinions/rhousing02. htm (accessed 28 November 2012).

19 AIR 1997 SC 152.

20 AIR 1990 SC 630.

it is the bare protection of the body; for a human being, it has to be a suitable accommodation, which would allow him [or her] to grow in every aspect—physical, mental and intellectual . . . It is not necessary that every citizen must be ensured of living in a well-built, comfortable house, but a reasonable home, particularly for people in India, can even be a mud-built thatched house or a mud-built fireproof accommodation.

Olga Tellis highlighted the connection between the right to livelihood (said to fall within the sweep of Article 21) and the proximity of slums to the workplace. Hence, the right to shelter was constitutionally protected through its indirect but inevitable link with the right to livelihood. However, subsequent decisions (as cited previously) recognized that the right to housing was independently a part and parcel of the right to life.[21] In another case[22] involving the compulsory acquisition of land to provide housing for Scheduled Castes (SC), the court specifically rejected the argument that when the right to livelihood was intertwined with the right to occupy land, the land could not be acquired by the state. The precedential value of *Olga Tellis* was not significantly tarnished by this case, since the 'right to livelihood' argument was invoked by powerful landowners against a social justice endeavour—a proposition which, if accepted by the court, would defeat the very substratum on which it was built.

Another notable consequence of *Olga Tellis* was that several concepts outlined by the Supreme Court, including a bright-line

21 *P.G. Gupta v. State of Gujarat* (1995 Supp (2) SCC 182).

22 *Chameli Singh v. State of Uttar Pradesh* (1996 (2) SCC 549); also *see* Hohmann, 'Visions of Social Transformation', p. 135.

'cut-off date'[23] and the right to rehabilitation, were accorded statutory recognition under the (amended) Maharashtra Slum Areas (Improvement, Clearance and Redevelopment) Act, 1971.

The Largest Court-Sanctioned Eviction in the World

In the years that followed, there was a symbolic shift in the Supreme Court's approach towards the displacement of disadvantaged sections of society and their fundamental right to shelter. In 1994, the Narmada Bachao Andolan (NBA), an NGO led by social activists including Medha Patkar, filed a writ petition in the Supreme Court seeking a restraint on the construction of the Sardar Sarovar Dam on the Narmada river. The NBA underscored the forced displacement of lakhs of tribal and rural families in the Narmada Valley (who were opposed to being rehabilitated) as well as serious environmental degradation as the grounds for halting the ambitious project. Initially, the court presented a ray of hope to human rights activists by admitting the petition and issuing a stay on the further construction of the dam. Construction remained in abeyance until 1999.

In 2000, the Supreme Court allowed the dam height to be raised and authorized its phased construction—in disregard of its own decisions in *Olga Tellis* and several other cases emphasizing the significance of the right to shelter. Granting compensation and rehabilitation to the displaced, the court reasoned that the displacement of tribals and other persons on account of

---

23 Regarding slum rehabilitation projects, occupants had the right of rehabilitation if they had moved into the hutment before the cut-off date. Such occupants would be entitled to free alternative housing whereas occupants who had moved in after the cut-off date would have to pay a transfer fee. In Maharashtra, the cut-off dates were 1 January 1995 and 1 January 2000, in respect of the different phases of the vital projects.

construction would not 'per se result in the violation of their fundamental or other rights'.[24] The court's simplistic and myopic approach was evident in its assertions that, after rehabilitation, the tribals would be in a better position than they were already in and they would have 'better amenities than which they enjoyed in their tribal hamlets'.[25] Apart from contravening established precedent, the Supreme Court's decision appeared to offer moral rather than legal grounds for the displacement of the tribals.

By allowing construction of the dam, the court took the number of persons displaced by the project to a staggering 3,20,000,[26] affixing its stamp of approval on the largest court-sanctioned forced eviction in the world.[27] Starting from 1999, the Supreme Court, from time to time, allowed the height of the dam to be increased. Most recently, on 8 May 2006, the Supreme Court allowed the height of the dam to be increased to 121.92 metres. But, ironically, reports, including one dated as recent as 31 October 2010, suggest that over 2,00,000 people affected by the construction of the Sardar Sarovar Dam still remain under constant threat of flooding and are yet to be compensated.[28]

---

24 *Narmada Bachao Andolan v. Union of India* (AIR 2000 SC 3751).

25 Ibid.

26 Joseph Hobbs and Andrew Dolan, *World Regional Geography*, 6th ed. (Belmont: Brooks/Cole, 2006), p. 319.

27 Balakrishnan Rajagopal, 'Pro-Human Rights but Anti-Poor?: A Critical Evaluation of the Indian Supreme Court from a Social Movement Perspective', *Human Rights Review*, vol. 18(3): pp. 157–87, http://ssrn.com/abstract=1013656 (accessed 15 February 2013).

28 Eric Randolph, 'Indian protest over Narmada dam builds awareness of rights', *The National*, 31 October 2010, www.thenational.ae/news/worldwide/south-asia/indian-protest-over-narmada-dam-builds-awareness-of   rights?pageCount=0 (accessed 15 February 2013).

'Encroacher: A Pickpocket?' And Third Generation Rights

A telling indicator of the significant transition in the attitude of Indian courts towards slum/pavement dwellers and encroachers is the harsh and insensitive language used by courts in recent times. The Supreme Court touched its lowest point in *Almitra Patel v. Union of India*.[29] Almitra Patel, a resident of Kothnur village, Bangalore, filed a writ petition concerning the inadequate solid waste management facilities in Delhi. In its judgement, the court said that providing alternative accommodation to slum/pavement dwellers was comparable to rewarding a pickpocket, and suggested that 'land grabbers' should be dealt with with an iron fist.

Interestingly, this case also reflects a drift in the focus of the Supreme Court with the emergence of what are loosely described as 'third generation rights', including the right to a clean and healthy environment and intergenerational equity. Faced with a clash between second and third generation rights, the Supreme Court has often allowed the latter to prevail over the former, without making serious attempts to reconcile the two. This is one of the reasons why the Supreme Court has been described as 'pro human rights but anti-poor'[30] in recent times.

Right to Housing in 21st-Century India

Even as Indian courts have digressed from the approach adopted in *Olga Tellis*, constitutional instruments and courts in other parts of the world have recognized that the state is duty-bound

---

29 (2000) 2 SCC 166.

30 Rajagopal, 'Pro-Human Rights but Anti-Poor?', pp. 157–87.

to devise and implement coherent programmes to provide decent housing. The constitutions of Argentina, Brazil and South Africa impose an obligation upon the government to provide adequate shelter to its citizens. One of the most significant decisions in the context of the right to shelter was made in *Government of the Republic of South Africa v. Grotboom*.[31] Hundreds of people living in atrocious conditions, as they awaited allocation of subsidized housing, petitioned the Constitutional Court of South Africa for temporary shelter. The court found that the state's housing programmes failed to meet the constitutional demand of providing access to adequate housing. As the Supreme Court of India had done in *Olga Tellis*, rather than granting immediate relief to the parties before it, the South African court also focused on rectifying the broader defects in the state housing policy.

Courts acting alone cannot tackle the challenge of slum redevelopment and rehabilitation. They need the support of well-executed social welfare policies and economic development strategies.[32] Taking slum/pavement dwellers into confidence via an inclusive and participatory process[33] would be an advisable approach to ensure the progressive realization of the right to housing as an inalienable right. That said, how the courts treat slum/pavement dwellers also significantly affects the attitude of policymakers and the society in general. In the years to come, Indian courts will be called upon to achieve a harmonious

---

31 [2000] ZACC 19.

32 *See* Ellen Wiles, 'Aspirational Principles or Enforceable Rights? The Future for Socio-Economic Rights in National Law', *American University International Law Review*, vol. 22 (2006): p. 35.

33 *See* Caroline Humphrey and Katherine Verdery, *Property in Question: Value Transformation in the Global Economy* (New York: Berg, 2004), p. 242.

balance between the right to shelter, a wholesome environment, economic development and a sustainable ecosystem.

Although *Olga Tellis* has not been formally overruled, its scope and effect have been significantly weakened from 1990 onwards. Yet, as a Constitution-Bench judgement of one of the most powerful courts in the world, it still acts as a strong reminder that the court will not remain a silent spectator when the human rights of the lowest rungs of society are about to be trampled upon.

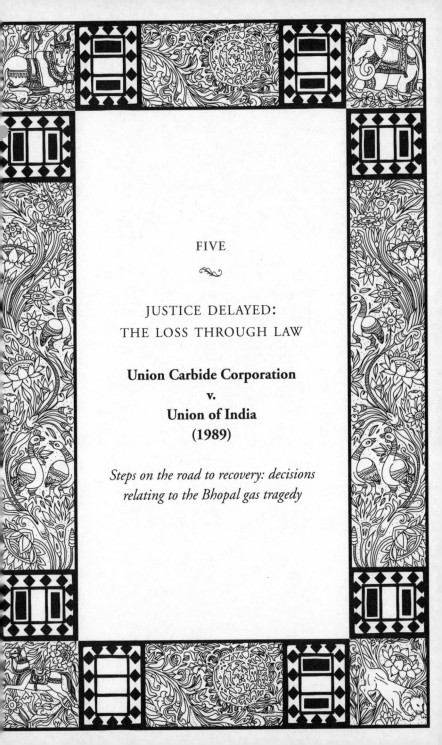

FIVE

JUSTICE DELAYED:
THE LOSS THROUGH LAW

**Union Carbide Corporation
v.
Union of India
(1989)**

*Steps on the road to recovery: decisions
relating to the Bhopal gas tragedy*

IN 1934, UNION Carbide India Ltd (UCIL) was incorporated in India to manufacture batteries, chemicals, pesticides and other industrial products. The American enterprise, Union Carbide Corporation (UCC) owned a majority stake in UCIL. In 1970, UCIL erected a pesticide plant in a densely populated area of Bhopal, Madhya Pradesh.

At the inception stage, UCC's Argentine agronomic engineer expressed concerns over the plant's safety, but his superiors disregarded them, saying that the plant would be 'as inoffensive as a chocolate factory'.[1] With approval from the Government of India, UCIL manufactured the pesticides Sevin and Temik in its Bhopal plant. On the night of 2–3 December 1984, water seeped into a tank containing over forty tonnes of the highly poisonous methyl isocyanate (MIC), a gas used in the production of Sevin and Temik.[2] This caused an exothermic reaction because of which the MIC escaped into the atmosphere—and when the northwesterlies blew this gas over the hutments adjacent to the

---

1 Rakesh Bhatnagar, 'Did UCC mislead India while seeking licence?', *DNA*, 5 July 2010, http://www.dnaindia.com/india/1405358/column-did-ucc-mislead-india-while-seeking-licence.

2 Although there are several theories regarding why water seeped into the MIC tank—*see* Sheila Jasanoff, 'The Bhopal Disaster Approaches 25: Looking Back to Look Forward: Bhopal's Trials of Knowledge and Ignorance', *New England Law Review*, vol. 42 (2008): p. 679—the most prominent among them attributes it to negligence on the part of UCIL. UCIL consistently contended that the said water seepage was caused by an act of sabotage by a disgruntled employee.

plant and into the very densely populated parts of Bhopal, the city was transformed into a 'gas chamber'.[3] As many as 2600 people died in the immediate wake of the leak, and the death toll rose to 8000 within a fortnight,[4] while hundreds of thousands were impacted. Bhopal had found a place on the world map for all the wrong reasons.

The ghosts of December 1984 haunted several generations of Bhopal's inhabitants. Over the next twenty-five years, although no official death count was undertaken, estimates indicate that the number of fatalities rose to a whopping 20,000 while 6,00,000 people suffered irreparable physical damage.[5] Many who were not even born at the time of the disaster but were still in the womb of their mothers endured its catastrophic consequences. Even today, residents of Bhopal suffer from genetic defects such as damaged reproductive systems, lung problems and vision impairments due to the gas leak that occurred almost three decades ago.[6]

The Bhopal gas tragedy remains unparalleled in the history of industrial disasters anywhere in the world.[7] What followed

---

3   Brad Schweiger, 'Safety vs. Security: How Broad but Selective Public Access to Environmental Data Properly Balances Communities' Safety and Homeland Security', *The John Marshall Journal of Computer and Information Law*, vol. 25 (2008): p. 273.

4   Ingrid Eckerman, 'Bhopal Gas Catastrophe 1984: Causes and Consequences' in *Encyclopedia of Environmental Health*, vol. 1, ed. Jerome Nriag (Burlington Elsevier, 2011), pp. 302–16.

5   Randeep Ramesh, 'Bhopal marks 25th anniversary of Union Carbide gas disaster', *The Guardian*, 3 December 2009, http://www.guardian.co.uk/world/2009/dec/03/bhopal-anniversary-union-carbide-gas (accessed 24 January 2013).

6   Sukanya Pillay, 'Absence of Justice: Lessons from the Bhopal Union Carbide Disaster for Latin America', *Michigan State Journal of International Law*, vol. 14 (2006): p. 479.

7   B.K. Khanna, *All You Wanted To Know About Disasters* (New Delhi: New India Publishing Agency, 2005), p. 155.

the accident was as regrettable as the incident itself. The Indian polity, judiciary, legal fraternity and the media squandered numerous opportunities to lay down a stern deterrent for those who believed that they could wantonly evade punishment for crimes committed in developing nations. In the years that followed, in their struggle for justice, the victims of the disaster were re-victimized.[8] There was a series of debates and decisions on several issues—ranging from the compensation payable to the victims, the criminal negligence of UCIL the piercing of the corporate veil,[9] the criminal liability of directors of UCIL and UCC, and the appropriate choice of forum[10]—in India as well as the United States of America, but little good trickled down to the victims of this catastrophe.

Parens Patriae and the Bhopal Gas Leak Disaster Act, 1985

At the time of the disaster, UCIL's ownership structure was such that UCC owned 51 per cent of the company, Life

---

8 Upendra Baxi, *Inconvenient Forum and Convenient Catastrophe* (Bombay: Indian Law Institute, 1986), p. 2.

9 'Piercing the corporate veil' is a legal concept. A company as an entity is separate from the people who promote and run it. As a result, any liability to a company is not a liability to its directors, promoters, or employees. Similarly, under law, a parent company is a separate entity from its subsidiary company and the liability to a subsidiary company is not, ordinarily, a liability to its parent. These features—of 'separate personality' of a company and 'limited liability' of the persons or entities associated with a company—have together made the corporation the most popular form of business organization. However, in certain circumstances, such as when the company is set up merely as a front to evade taxes or to perpetrate fraud, courts 'pierce the corporate veil' and ignore the separate corporate personality of a company to find out the people who are really running the company. In such cases, courts also ignore the 'limited liability' of persons associated with companies and make such persons fully liable for acts of the company.

10 'Choice of forum' refers to the place where a legal action is initiated.

Insurance Corporation of India/Unit Trust of India owned 22 per cent and the Indian public owned 27 per cent.[11] Soon after the leak, hundreds of tort lawyers from the United States of America and their Indian counterparts descended on Bhopal, seeking exemplary damages for those affected by the tragedy (and retaining some of those damages for themselves).[12] The Government of India was quick to derail their hopes. It promulgated the Bhopal Gas Leak Disaster (Processing of Claims) Ordinance, 1985, which was replaced by the Bhopal Gas Leak Disaster (Processing of Claims) Act, 1985 (the Bhopal Act) on 29 March 1985. The Bhopal Act gave the Central government the exclusive right to represent and act (in India or overseas) in place of the persons entitled to make claims in relation to the Bhopal gas leak. It authorized the Central government to represent the interests of those affected by the gas leak as 'parens patriae'—this tool, which originated in the United Kingdom and evolved in the United States of America,[13] allows the state to protect the well-being of its citizens in a representative capacity.

The Bhopal Act evoked sharp criticism, as the wrongdoer (UCIL) was partly owned by state corporations and the government could have been held partially liable for the tragedy. By invoking parens patriae, the government began to represent the very victims who could have initiated action against it. The government's action has therefore been criticized as a device

---

11 Approximate figures, in the sense that UCC owned 50.99 per cent of UCIL, rounded off accordingly. At the time, the maximum investment permissible for a foreign investor was 40 per cent. However, the Central government waived this requirement on account of the sophistication of its technology and UCC's potential for export; *see* Khanna, *All You Wanted To Know About Disasters*, p. 156.

12 Jasanoff, 'The Bhopal Disaster Approaches 25', p. 679.

13 Lisa Moscati Hawkes, 'Parens Patriae and the Union Carbide Case: The Disaster at Bhopal Continues', *Cornell International Law Journal*, vol. 21 (1988): p. 181.

meant to protect itself from culpability for the Bhopal gas leak rather than protect its victims.[14] The constitutional validity of the Bhopal Act was also challenged before the Supreme Court.[15] Justifying the application of the parens patriae principle, the court held:

> The government is within its duty to protect and to control persons under disability. Conceptually, the parens patriae theory is the obligation of the state to protect and take into custody the rights and the privileges of its citizens for discharging its obligations. Our Constitution makes it imperative for the state to secure to all its citizens the rights guaranteed by the Constitution and where the citizens are not in a position to assert and secure their rights, the state must come into picture and protect and fight for the rights of the citizens.[16]

Even though it was tenuous, parens patriae could have been an effective mechanism to obtain a speedy remedy only if the government had pursued it with conviction and while bearing in mind the interest of the victims. However, the government did not match its power with 'results or responsibility'.[17] The outcome was that the victims were double-crossed by the state—they were left with little compensation and also deprived of their right to act in their individual capacities.

14 Themistocles D'Silva, *The Black Box of Bhopal: A Closer Look at the World's Deadliest Industrial Disaster* (Victoria, B.C.: Trafford, 2006), p. 151.

15 *Charan Lal Sahu v. Union of India* (AIR 1990 SC 1480).

16 Ibid.

17 Sriram Panchu, 'Bhopal gas leak case: all is not lost', *The Hindu*, 19 June 2010, http://www.thehindu.com/opinion/lead/bhopal-gas-leak-case-all-is-not-lost/article472555.ece.

Proceedings before the Keenan Court

Exercising its powers under the Bhopal Act, on 8 April 1985, the Central government filed a complaint against UCC before the Southern District Court in New York, United States of America.[18] By then, 144 proceedings were already under way in federal courts across the United States in respect of the Bhopal gas leak. All these proceedings were consolidated and assigned to the court of Judge John Keenan.[19] The arguments projected a strange situation—the Union of India argued that Indian courts could not handle the matter efficaciously while a United States corporation asserted that they could. India 'biopsied' its own legal system while an American corporation celebrated it![20]

Acting on behalf of the victims, the Indian government stated the following:[21]

1. India's legal system was ill-equipped to handle the complex litigation that the case would entail.

2. The endemic delays in India's legal system and the substantial backlog of cases would impede the effective disposal of the case.

3. Indian lawyers could not provide proper representation due to a lack of expertise in the area of tort claims.

---

18 The Central government's decision to sue UCC in a US district court was criticized as one laced with ulterior motives (*see* Sudhir K. Chopra, 'Multinational Corporations in the Aftermath Of Bhopal: The Need For A New Comprehensive Global Regime For Transnational Corporate Activity', *Valparaiso University Law Review*, vol. 29 (1994): p. 235).

19 *In re: Union Carbide Corporation Gas Plant Disaster at Bhopal, India in December, 1984* ((1986) 634 F. Supp. 842).

20 Baxi, *Inconvenient Forum and Convenient Catastrophe*, p. 1.

21 Peter J. Carney, 'International Forum Non Conveniens: "Section 1404.5": A Proposal in the Interest of Sovereignty, Comity, and Individual Justice', *American University Law Review*, vol. 45 (1995): p. 415.

4. Tort law in India was not developed enough to deal with a case of such gigantic proportions.
5. Procedural law in India would hinder the path of justice for the victims.

The court extensively discussed whether Indian courts were competent to grapple with the Bhopal disaster case. Judge Keenan concluded that the arguments were untenable and dismissed the claim on the ground of *forum non conveniens*—a doctrine based on which a court can refuse jurisdiction over a case where a more appropriate/convenient forum is available. The court held that most of the documentary evidence concerning the plant's design, safety and setup was in India, as were the vast majority of witnesses who had to be examined. Moreover, the Indian government had an 'extensive and deep interest'[22] in ensuring compliance with safety standards. Judge Keenan believed that India's interest in developing minimum standards of care was superior to the United States's interest in deterring multinationals from exporting dangerous technology to other nations. Strikingly, Judge Keenan made certain politically flavoured (and, to an extent, patronizing) observations on the potential of Indian courts to dispense justice:

To retain the litigation in this forum . . . would be yet another example of imperialism, another situation in which an established sovereign inflicted its rules, its standards and values on a developing nation. This court declines to play such a role. The Union of India is a world power in 1986, and its courts

---

22 Carney, 'International Forum Non Conveniens', p. 415.

have the proven capacity to mete out fair and equal justice. To deprive the Indian judiciary of this opportunity to stand tall before the world and to pass judgement on behalf of its own people would be to revive a history of subservience and subjugation from which India has emerged. India and its people can and must vindicate their claims before the independent and legitimate judiciary created there since the Independence of 1947.[23]

The dismissal of the Union of India's case was subject to three conditions:

1. UCC would have to consent to submit to the jurisdiction of Indian courts and continue to waive defences founded on the statute of limitations.[24]

2. UCC would have to abide by any judgement rendered by an Indian court as long as it complied with 'minimal' due process[25] requirements.

3. After an appropriate demand by the Union of India, UCC was to be subject to discovery[26] under the model of the United States's Federal Rules of Civil Procedure.

---

23 Carney, 'International Forum Non Conveniens', p. 415.

24 'Limitation' is a legal concept that sets a time limit within which legal proceedings can be commenced. It seeks to make legal actions finite by ensuring that people can only commence legal proceedings within a certain period of time and not thereafter.

25 'Due process' refers to the procedure a court or other administrative body follows in order to arrive at a decision. It requires that no judgement must be pronounced against a person without informing the person of the case against him/her and giving him/her an opportunity to defend himself/herself. It also requires the court or administrative body to be impartial, fair, just and reasonable (*see* P. Ramanatha Aiyar, *Advanced Law Lexicon* (New Delhi: LexisNexis Butterworths Wadhwa Nagpur, 2009), p. 1504).

26 'Discovery' is the process of obtaining information from the opposing party before trial in a lawsuit (*see* Aiyar, *Advanced Law Lexicon*, p. 1409).

Judge Keenan's decision was ironic—the great opportunity that he believed India's legal system faced was (as we will examine later in this chapter) squandered by the bar and the bench.

Back in India, the Meagre Settlement

So, in September 1986, the Union of India instituted proceedings against UCC in a district court in Bhopal, which ordered UCC to deposit an interim compensation of 350 crore (3.5 billion) rupees. On appeal, the Madhya Pradesh High Court reduced the figure to 250 crore (2.5 billion) rupees. UCC appealed to the Supreme Court of India against the high court's decision. Although, under Indian law, a judgement debtor is supposed to deposit the contested amount before moving an appellate court, UCC did not do so.[27]

Aiming to dispense speedy justice to the victims, the court ordered UCC to pay 470 million dollars (approximately 750 crore [7.5 billion] rupees then) 'in full settlement of all claims, rights and liabilities related to and arising out of the Bhopal gas disaster'.[28] The compensation amount was a mean between UCC's offer of 426 million dollars and the Union of India's demand for 500 million dollars. In terms of the settlement, all civil proceedings were concluded and criminal proceedings quashed in relation to the Bhopal gas leak. Although the five-judge Constitution Bench of the Supreme Court passed this order on Valentine's Day in 1989, the victims had no great affection for the order, since the Central government had earlier kindled their hopes of obtaining

27 Pillay, 'Absence of Justice: Lessons from the Bhopal Union Carbide Disaster', p. 479.
28 *Union Carbide Corporation v. Union of India and Others* ((1989) 1 SCC 674).

compensation amounting to 3 billion dollars—more than six times the final settlement amount. Several NGOs also expressed widespread dissatisfaction over the settlement.[29]

A few months later, the Supreme Court issued a reasoned decision for its order granting compensation to the victims.[30] One of the unfortunate effects of the settlement was that the court did not adjudicate on the critical issues raised by the Bhopal incident, though it stated its observations on the need to protect national interests from being exploited by foreign corporations and develop criteria to deal with potentially hazardous technology. The Supreme Court reiterated that the compensation was adequate and that it actually exceeded personal injury claims at the time.[31] It clearly failed to appreciate the extent of the damage caused by the Bhopal gas leak and its crippling long-term effects. (To put things into perspective, if we take a conservative estimate that 1,70,000 people were killed or injured in the disaster, each victim/kin would get less than 50,000 rupees as compensation.)

Indian law does not value life as much as it is valued in other nations, such as the United States of America. Is it because we have so many people that each one doesn't mean as much?

Criminal Charges Revived

The settlement sanctioned by the Supreme Court was widely condemned. A few years after its 1989 settlement order, the

29 Fali S. Nariman, *Before Memory Fades: An Autobiography* (New Delhi: Hay House, 2010), pp. 205–06.

30 *Union Carbide Corporation v. Union of India and Others* ((1989) 3 SCC 38).

31 Ibid.

Supreme Court clubbed several petitions filed against the order and formed a five-judge Constitution Bench to hear arguments challenging the basis of the settlement. (In exceptional cases, the Supreme Court has the power to review its own judgements, under Article 137 of the Constitution.) However, before the judgement could be pronounced, the then Chief Justice of India, Justice Sabyasachi Mukherjee, passed away. This necessitated a rehearing, which caused further delays. In its judgement dated 3 October 1991, the court finally recognized the legal sanctity of the order recording the settlement between UCC and the Union of India. It wasted the opportunity of revising the 470-million-dollar compensation to a more realistic figure. The court also emphasized the need to grant speedy justice to the victims—by its own calculation, the full adjudication of the suits relating to the Bhopal disaster would have taken till 2010.[32]

The judgement did have two positive consequences. First, it catalysed the condemnation of the quashing of the criminal process against the UCC officers and revival of criminal proceedings against them. Second, the court held that if the settlement amount fell short, the Union of India was bound to make good the shortfall. Remarkably, Justice Aziz Mushabber Ahmadi, who went on to become the Chief Justice of India in 1994, dissented on this point, questioning why the Indian taxpayer should be liable when the Union of India was neither held liable in tort for the disaster nor was shown to have acted negligently while entering into the settlement.[33]

---

32 *Union Carbide Corporation v. Union of India and Others* (AIR 1992 SC 248).
33 Ibid.

Oleum Gas Leak Case

Almost exactly a year after the Bhopal gas leak, there were two instances of leakage of oleum gas from a unit of Shriram Foods and Fertilizer Industries (Shriram) in Delhi. A handful of people were affected and one person even died as a result. However, with the Bhopal incident fresh in their minds, Delhi's citizens were understandably in a state of panic. The District Magistrate of Delhi responded by passing an order telling Shriram to stop manufacturing and processing toxic chemicals and gases. M.C. Mehta filed a writ petition in the Supreme Court concerning the norms that should be used to determine the liability of organizations engaged in manufacturing and selling hazardous materials.[34] The first question before the court, however, was whether Shriram's caustic chlorine plant should have been allowed to restart operations simply because it employed over 4000 people. A three-judge bench permitted the plant to restart subject to eleven prescribed conditions. The other questions raised involved issues of constitutional significance and were referred to a five-judge bench of the court.

Until *M.C. Mehta v. Union of India*,[35] the English principle of strict liability laid down in *Rylands v. Fletcher*[36] was the law governing industrial accidents in India. According to this principle, a person who introduces anything hazardous—likely to harm people and property should it escape—to his land, must do so at his own peril. He would be prima facie answerable for all damage caused by the natural consequences of such escape of

34 *M.C. Mehta v. Union of India* (AIR 1987 SC 965).

35 *M.C. Mehta v. Union of India* (AIR 1987 SC 1086).

36 [1868] UKHL 1.

hazardous material. Over the years, this rule was diluted by several exceptions—including a natural calamity, an act of sabotage and consent of the plaintiff—carved out by English courts.[37] A five-judge bench of the Supreme Court increased the threshold of tortious liability when it held that an enterprise engaging in any harmful or inherently dangerous activity had an absolute and 'non-delegable' duty to ensure that no one was harmed, and if anyone was harmed, they were to be compensated.[38] In asserting this duty, the Supreme Court did not accept the exceptions which had evolved in English jurisprudence.

This ruling was significant in that the Supreme Court coupled Indian seasoning with English principles to regulate an environment in which industrial growth was not matched with necessary legal reform.

Criminal Proceedings against the UCC and UCIL Officers

After the criminal proceedings against the directors and officers of UCC and UCIL recommenced,[39] many criminal cases did the rounds in courts across India. Initially, charges were framed against the accused under Section 304 of the Indian Penal Code (the IPC) for culpable homicide not amounting to murder—an offence punishable by imprisonment for a maximum of ten years. Responding to an appeal, the Supreme Court diluted the charge to 'causing death by negligence' under Section 304A

---

37 V. Venkatesan, 'Bhopal Gas Disaster: Judicial Failure', *Frontline*, 19 December 2009–1 January 2010.

38 *M.C. Mehta v. Union of India* (AIR 1987 SC 1086).

39 *Union Carbide Corporation v. Union of India and Others* (AIR 1992 SC 248); discussed earlier.

of the IPC (which provided for punishment by imprisonment up to two years only) on the ground that the evidence was not sufficient to charge the accused with culpable homicide.[40] The trial proceeded in the Chief Judicial Magistrate's court, and on 7 June 2010, seven people were convicted for two years each in connection with the Bhopal gas leak.[41] Warren Anderson, Chairman of UCC at the time of the leak, did not appear in court and was declared an absconder. Though the court slapped the maximum punishment it could, it was sharply criticized for treating the disaster like a 'minor traffic accident'.[42]

Give to the Rich and Rob from the Poor?

The Bhopal gas leak was cited by many as a paradigm of how influential multinationals exploit developing countries;[43]— developing countries import hazardous technology in spite of a conspicuous absence of an environmental law framework[44] and legal infrastructure to handle its potentially disastrous consequences. The most ironic aspect of globalization in the 1980s and '90s was that in their quest for economic development, developing nations sacrificed the human rights

---

40 *Keshub Mahindra v. State of M.P.* ((1996) 6 SCC 129).

41 *State of M.P. v. Warren Anderson and Others*, Cr. Case No. 8460/1996, Chief Judicial Magistrate of Bhopal, judgement delivered on 7 June 2010.

42 'Bhopal disaster and the BP oil spill', *The Hindu*, 4 August 2010, http://www.thehindu.com/opinion/op-ed/bhopal-disaster-and-the-bp-oil-spill/article550062.ece.

43 *See* Jasanoff, 'The Bhopal Disaster Approaches 25', p. 679, where the author refers to globalization as a phenomenon that is far from 'even-handed in its flows and frictions'.

44 Zakia Afrin, 'Foreign Direct Investments and Sustainable Development in the Least-Developed Countries', *Annual Survey of International and Comparative Law*, vol. 10 (2004): p. 215.

of the lowest rungs of their societies. Foreign companies were accused of committing some of the most heinous crimes—from homicide and rape to forced labour.[45] Bhopal was undoubtedly the darkest reflection of globalization.[46] It forced citizens to seriously weigh the costs of globalization against its benefits, particularly when modern technology was imported into an archaic legal set-up, as was the case with India.

Bhopal and BP

In 2010, an oil spill of unprecedented magnitude occurred in the Gulf of Mexico when a mobile offshore drilling unit, which was drilling an exploratory well, exploded and leaked out close to 5 million barrels of crude oil. Within weeks of the incident, BP—the corporation held responsible for the spill—created a 20 billion-dollar fund to deal with the accident. Within two years and four days of the incident, federal investigators in the United States of America made their first arrest in the matter.[47]

The incidents in the Gulf of Mexico and Bhopal were acutely distinct: the former wreaked massive environmental destruction, the latter decimated thousands of humans and deprived thousands more of the basic quality of life. The former also took place at a time when environmental law was more equipped to handle mass disasters. At the same time, one cannot help but

---

45 Pillay, 'Absence of Justice: Lessons from the Bhopal Union Carbide Disaster', p. 479.

46 Roda Mushkat, 'Globalization and the International Environmental Legal Response: The Asian Context', *University of Hawaii Asian-Pacific Law and Policy Journal*, vol. 4 (2003): p. 3.

47 'Former BP engineer arrested on U.S. criminal charges related to gulf oil spill', *The Washington Post*, 24 April 2012, http://articles.washingtonpost.com/2012-04-24/business/35453534_1_kurt-mix-bp-executives-spill-disaster (accessed 12 February 2013).

notice the differential treatment of the two incidents. Had the accident occurred in Indian waters, would BP have paid even half the compensation it eventually did?

Have We Learnt Our Lessons from Bhopal?

The Bhopal gas disaster jolted lackadaisical politicians and policymakers. Before 1984, India only had specific legislation pertinent to air and water pollution.[48] After the Bhopal tragedy, however, India enacted the Environment Protection Act (1986), a statute that seeks to address pressing concerns involving sustainable development. This was followed up by the enactment of the Public Liability Insurance Act, 1991 and the National Environment Tribunal Act, 1995. The Environmental Impact Assessment Notification, which formulated an approval mechanism for industrial projects, was also passed on 27 January 1994 (and subsequently amended from time to time).[49] All this worked to raise the enviro-consciousness of Indian citizens by several notches.

However, despite all the environmental legislation, there is still a definite lacuna in the Indian legal structure. On 6 July 2011, the UN General Assembly adopted the 'Guiding Principles on Business and Human Rights: Implementing the United Nations "Protect, Respect and Remedy" Framework' (the UN Framework), a report by Harvard Law School professor and

---

48 Sanjay Jose Mullick, 'Power Game in India: Environmental Clearance and the Enron Project', *Stanford Environmental Law Journal*, vol. 16 (1997): p. 256.

49 Julie A. Lemmer, 'Cleaning up Development: EIA in Two of the World's Largest and Most Rapidly Developing Countries', *Georgetown International Environmental Law Review*, vol. 19 (2007): p. 275.

United Nations Special Representative John Ruggie. As per the UN Framework, governments must clearly spell out their policies to protect human rights and communicate these to business organizations. Further, businesses must undertake regular human rights impact assessment (HRIA) and due diligence, and create internal policies to ensure compliance with human rights norms. However, despite the UN Framework, Indian law does not yet clearly spell out any such requirements for corporations. The National Voluntary Guidelines on Social, Environmental and Economic Responsibilities of Businesses[50] do enjoin companies to 'respect and promote human rights' and to 'respect, promote and make efforts to restore the environment', but these guidelines are non-binding. All they entail are filing requirements, and that too, only for the top 100 companies in terms of market capitalization.[51]

So, despite the government's steps in the aftermath of Bhopal, there is still room for a substantial number of measures to be still undertaken. In the realm of corporate law, the (Indian) Companies Act, 1956 could be amended to reflect the UN Framework. While the proposed new Companies Bill (which will eventually replace the Companies Act of 1956) introduces the concept of corporate social responsibility committees,[52] it would be more effective to introduce a clause to escalate an

---

50 Issued by the Ministry of Corporate Affairs, Government of India, www.mca.gov. in/Ministry/latestnews/National_Voluntary_Guidelines_2011_12jul2011.pdf (accessed 12 February 2013).

51 Securities and Exchange Board of India, press release no. 145/2011, 24 November 2011, www.sebi.gov.in/sebiweb/home/detail/22104/yes/PR-SEBI-Board-meeting (accessed 12 February 2013).

52 Ministry of Corporate Affairs, proposed Section 135 of the Companies Bill, www. mca.gov.in/Ministry/pdf/The_Companies_Bill_2012.pdf (accessed 12 February 2012).

HRIA and stakeholder consultation to the level of directorial duties. This would give victims an enforceable remedy, going beyond the 'name and shame' approach. Further, as a matter of policy, the government could also consider 'buying social justice'[53] by incorporating due diligence and HRIA obligations into government contracts awarded to private entities. Finally, the Protection of Human Rights Act, 1993, which governs human rights commissions in India, should be broadened to cover violations even by non-state actors.

The recent Civil Liability for Nuclear Damage Bill, 2010 (passed by both houses of Parliament) caps the liability of nuclear plant operators for nuclear accidents to 1500 crore (15 billion) rupees (roughly 325 million dollars). This amount is lower than the 470-million-dollar compensation awarded in the Bhopal case, which in itself was grossly insufficient. The proposed framework of nuclear liability law has created a dangerous cocktail for another Bhopal. It reinforces the fact that justice in India is still administered reactively, not proactively.

Looking Ahead

It seems that the Bhopal debacle was not enough of a wake-up call for lawyers, judges, politicians, activists and the media. In fact, they appeared to have pressed the snooze button and gone on to repeat mistakes of the past. Bureaucracy and power dynamics worked together to cause unparalleled mental agony to the victims seeking justice. Some proceedings in respect of

---

53 Tanurabh Khaitan, 'Possibilities of Equality', *Indian Express*, 20 June 2008, http://www.indianexpress.com/news/possibilities-of-equality/325120/ (accessed 18 January 2013).

the Bhopal gas disaster are still pending in courts in the United States of America.[54]

Twenty-eight years on, neither the pursuit of criminal proceedings nor the enhancement of the compensation figures will vindicate the suffering of the Bhopal victims and their families. Yet, additional compensation packages can be the balm to soothe the wounds of the thousands who still suffer physically, emotionally and financially—as a consequence of that fateful December night. The 1265-crore-rupee (12.65-billion-rupee) aid package cleared by the Union Cabinet for the Bhopal victims in 2010 is a step in the right direction. The curative petition moved by the Central government before the Supreme Court, seeking an additional compensation of 7844 crore (78.44 billion) rupees,[55] is a more realistic and appropriate amount with which to compensate the victims, being closer to the monetary figure of the actual and total damage. How much of the promised amount will actually reach those for whom it is intended still remains to be seen. The Achilles' heel of Indian policy is exposed.

---

54 *Sahu and Others v. Union Carbide Corporation and Others* ((2007) 475 F.3d 465).

55 Sanjay K. Singh, 'Bhopal tragedy: Govt asks for Rs 7,844 cr more for victims', *The Economic Times*, 4 December 2010, http://articles.economictimes. indiatimes.com/2010-12-04/news/27628406_1_dow-chemicals-dow-chemicals-compensation (accessed 28 November 2012).

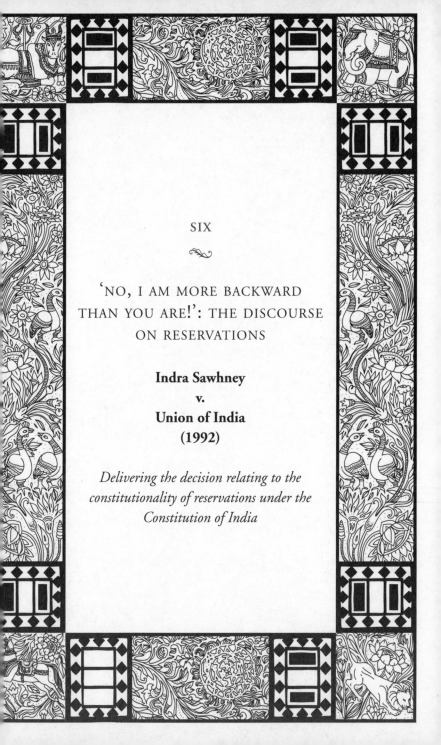

SIX

'NO, I AM MORE BACKWARD
THAN YOU ARE!': THE DISCOURSE
ON RESERVATIONS

Indra Sawhney
v.
Union of India
(1992)

*Delivering the decision relating to the
constitutionality of reservations under the
Constitution of India*

INDIA'S POLICY OF reservations is an issue that almost every Indian born post Independence ponders over, criticizes, utilizes, or suffers from at some stage in life. The expression 'reservations'—alternatively referred to as 'affirmative action' or 'positive discrimination' or 'compensatory discrimination'[1]—refers to justice granted to persons belonging to historically disadvantaged groups. In India, reservations mandated by the Constitution are implemented in the form of percentage-based quotas favouring citizens from traditionally lower rungs of society.

In India, reservation is closely linked to the caste system. Caste-based discrimination finds its genesis in the erstwhile varna system of the Hindus. Hindus were classified into four occupational tiers: Brahmins (scholars, priests, sages), Kshatriyas (warriors), Vaishyas (agriculturists, merchants) and Shudras (labourers, artisans, craftsmen). The first three groups comprised 'higher castes' while Shudras were considered to be from a 'low caste' background and not permitted to accumulate

---

1   Though these terms are often used interchangeably, there are subtle differences between them. 'Affirmative action' refers to policies that take factors such as race, colour, religion, gender and—in the Indian context—caste, into consideration to benefit an under-represented group in areas of employment, education and business. 'Positive discrimination', as it is known in the United Kingdom, is the process of giving preferential treatment to minority groups that have been prejudiced against in the past.

wealth.[2] Meanwhile, there were also the Dalits (earlier called 'untouchables'[3]) who were considered inferior beings and fell completely outside this four-fold classification—they were considered *avarna* or casteless. Most upper-caste Hindus shunned any form of contact with the Dalit community. Each of these castes is further classified into hundreds of hierarchically stratified sub-castes.

Reservations have had a chequered political history in the context of public employment and admissions to higher educational institutions. Joining the government service in India is considered, at least by the masses, to be a prestigious, stable occupation with a regular income—it offers job security, pension, and, in the case of senior officers, free housing.[4] With the liberalization of the Indian economy, the importance of citizens' educational background has overtaken their physical capital in the labour market. It is not surprising then that there is such a scramble to get sub-castes classified as 'backward', get fake caste certificates issued and have fraudulent income statements prepared. Today, nearly half a billion Indians are eligible to avail of some form of preferential treatment; the

---

2   Kevin D. Brown and Vinay Sitapati, 'Across Boundaries: Lessons Learned from Comparing the Application of Constitutional Law and Federal Anti-Discrimination Law to African-Americans in the US and Dalits in India in the Context of Higher Education', *Harvard Black Letter Law Journal*, vol. 24 (2008): p. 3.

3   Mahatma Gandhi used the term 'Harijans' to describe Dalits, while Dr B.R. Ambedkar, himself a Dalit and an architect of India's Constitution, preferred the expression 'Protestant Hindus'; *see* Dhananjay Keer, *Dr. Ambedkar: Life and Mission* (Mumbai: Popular Prakashan, 2005), p. 522.

4   E.J. Prior, 'Constitutional Fairness or Fraud on the Constitution? Compensatory Discrimination in India', *Case Western Reserve Journal of International Law*, vol. 28 (1996): p. 63.

count would be higher had it not been for the Supreme Court's periodic interventions.[5]

Backward communities in India are broadly divided into the following categories: (1) Scheduled Castes (SCs), comprising Dalits, (2) Scheduled Tribes (STs), comprising tribal communities living in isolated parts of India, and (3) Other Backward Classes (OBCs), identified as socially and economically backward.[6] Reservations for OBCs have been the most contentious and have caused a backlash in many parts of India. At the heart of this backlash was the Supreme Court's judgement in *Indra Sawhney v. Union of India*[7] (*Indra Sawhney*). It sought to reconcile the conflict between uplifting the poor while giving the criterion of 'merit' its due.

Reservations: From the British Raj to the Constitution of India

Way back in 1902, Shahu IV, the Maharaja of Kolhapur in Maharashtra, took the first organized step to provide reservations for backward classes in India. His aim was two-fold: eradicate poverty in the backward classes and increase their involvement in public administration.[8] The British took their cue and, from the early 1900s, developed religion- and caste-based policies of

---

5   George H. Gadbois, Jr, 'Mandal and the Other Backward Classes: Affirmative Action in India in the 1990s', *Journal of Law and Social Challenges*, vol. 1 (1997): p. 71.

6   Karthik Nagarajan, 'Compensatory Discrimination in India Sixty Years after Independence: A Vehicle of Progress or a Tool of Partisan Politics?', *Washington and Lee Journal of Civil Rights and Social Justice*, vol. 15 (2009): p. 483.

7   AIR 1993 SC 477.

8   Mehbubul Hassan Laskar, 'Rethinking Reservation in Higher Education in India', *ILI Law Review*, vol. 1, no. 1 (2010): p. 25.

reservation in the sphere of public governance—a tactic widely perceived as a centrepiece of their 'divide and rule' strategy.[9] For instance, the Indian Councils Act of 1909 (better known as the Morley–Minto reforms) provided separate electorates for Muslims and reserved seats in municipal and district boards, provincial councils and even in the legislature for India at the time. The Government of India Acts of 1919 and 1935 also had provisions for reservations.

These precursors to the Indian Constitution which entered into force in 1950, laid the foundation for an intricate reservation framework.[10] Although Article 14 of the Constitution gives to all people the right to equality before the law, Article 16(4) allows the state to make 'any provision for the reservation of appointments or posts' in favour of backward classes not represented adequately in services under the state. Article 46, a directive principle of state policy,[11] sets out that the state must promote the educational and economic interests of SCs and STs. Article 340 authorizes the President to form a commission to make recommendations for improving the conditions of backward classes. Articles 341 and 342 lay down the procedure to ascertain which castes and tribes should be considered as SCs and STs, respectively.[12]

---

9   Prior, 'Constitutional Fairness or Fraud on the Constitution?', p. 63.

10 The regime of reservations refers to that originally contemplated under the Constitution. Subsequently, there have been several constitutional amendments adding to the original framework.

11 An aspirational principle which, though not legally binding, is fundamental to India's governance.

12 For both SCs and STs, the President of India is authorized to specify the castes, races, tribes or groups to be categorized as SCs or STs for each state. The Parliament is empowered to modify the President's list.

The Constitution's provisions on reservation have been criticized as pro-Hindu, since the reservation policy was primarily aimed at abolishing the Hindu caste system.[13] Muslims have been sceptical of these constitutional principles because significant segments of disadvantaged Muslims have been unable to avail of the benefits of affirmative action in India.

Post-constitutional Developments

The first confrontation between the Parliament and the courts on the reservations issue took place just a year after the Constitution came into effect in 1950. Some colleges in Madras implemented detailed quota-based reservations, but the Supreme Court struck them down, explaining that the reservations, which were based on race, religion and caste, were opposed to Article 29(2) of the Constitution, which embodies a fundamental right which states that no citizen shall be denied admission into any educational institution maintained by the state or receiving aid out of state funds only on grounds of religion, race, caste, language or any of them.[14] In reaction, the Parliament amended Article 15[15] of the Constitution to allow the state to make special provisions for the advancement of socially and economically backward classes, SCs and STs.[16] By 1951, provisions for reservation in educational

13 Scott Grinsell, 'Caste and the Problem of Social Reform in Indian Equality Law', *The Yale Journal of International Law*, vol. 35 (2010): p. 199.

14 *State of Madras v. Champakam Dorairajan* (AIR 1951 SC 226).

15 Article 15 of the Constitution prohibits discrimination against citizens on the basis of religion, race, caste, sex or place of birth.

16 Article 15(4) of the Constitution, inserted by the Constitution (First Amendment) Act, 1951, reads: 'Nothing in this article or in clause (2) of article 29 [which prohibits denial of admission to educational institutions maintained by the State or receiving aid from State funds on the basis of caste and other factors] shall prevent

institutions and in public employment were constitutionally mandated, under Articles 15 and 16, respectively.

In 1953, the First Backward Classes Commission (1955), also known as the Kaka Kalelkar Commission, was formed under the chairmanship of Kaka Kalelkar, a social reformer and Rajya Sabha member, to make recommendations on how the position of backward classes in India could be enhanced (under the ambit of Article 340). Two years later, the commission identified 2399 backward groups on the basis of the following criteria: education, participation in public sector employment, trade and occupation, and—most significantly—position in the traditional Hindu caste system.[17] Kalelkar himself strongly disapproved of the commission's methodology and conclusions, underscoring the fact that undue emphasis on caste, as against economic indicators, would exclude destitute Muslims and Christians from the benefit of affirmative action, since Christianity and Islam do not have a caste system. The recommendations never saw the light of day. It was left up to the states to develop their own criteria to ascertain the groups for whom they would reserve quotas in education and public employment.[18]

The Supreme Court's supervisory role to monitor the extent of reservations in states across India began with the judgement

---

the State from making any special provision for the advancement of any socially and educationally backward classes of citizens or for the Scheduled Castes and the Scheduled Tribes.'

17 Katayoun Alidadi, 'Opening Doors to Muslim Minorities in the Workplace? From India's Employment Quota to EU and Belgian Anti-discrimination Legislation', *Pace International Law Review*, vol. 23 (2011): p. 146.

18 Clark Cunningham, Glenn Loury, and John Skrentny, 'Passing Strict Scrutiny: Using Social Science to Design Affirmative Action Programs', *Georgetown Law Journal*, vol. 90 (2002): p. 835.

in *M.R. Balaji v. State of Mysore*[19] (*Balaji*). In 1962, the state of Mysore (now Karnataka) issued an order reserving 68 per cent of the seats in engineering and medical colleges for SC, ST and OBC students. Twenty-three petitioners challenged this order, emphasizing that the extravagant quota was a fraud on the constitutional policy of reservations. Interpreting Articles 15(4) and 16(4) that deal with reservations in education and public employment, the Supreme Court balanced the competing interests of rewarding merit and uplifting the deprived classes by affirming that reservations should not usually exceed 50 per cent, since that would deprive meritorious candidates of a reasonable opportunity of admission/selection. It also said that while caste was an important criterion to ascertain social backwardness, it could not be the sole criterion, since religions other than Hinduism do not recognize caste-based distinctions. In later cases, it reiterated and developed some principles laid down in the *Balaji* decision.[20]

In 1975, in a subsequent case before the Supreme Court, although the *Balaji* decision was not overruled, a few judges opined that the extent of reservations may exceed 50 per cent in proportion with the actual population of backward classes.[21] While asserting that caste was the appropriate parameter to identify backwardness, the court in *K.C. Vasanth Kumar v. State of Karnataka*[22] also failed to conclude whether the 50 per cent reservation ceiling imposed in *Balaji* was applicable.

---

19 AIR 1963 SC 649.
20 Both *T. Devadasan v. Union of India* (AIR 1964 SC 179) and *Chitralekha v. State of Mysore* (AIR 1964 SC 1823) highlight that considering the caste of a group would not always be mandatory to ascertain backwardness.
21 *State of Kerala v. N.M. Thomas* (AIR 1976 SC 490).
22 AIR 1985 SC 1495.

Thus, by the late 1980s, there was rampant confusion and uncertainty regarding the constitutional boundaries of India's reservation policy. Would reservations above 50 per cent be considered unconstitutional? Would caste be the only criterion to determine the backwardness of communities? Could state governments take economic indicators into account while listing backward classes?

And Along Came the Mandal Commission

Over two decades after the first backward classes commission report was published, Prime Minister Morarji Desai fulfilled the Janata Party's electoral promise by constituting the second commission on backward classes in 1979. Set up under the chairmanship of B.P. Mandal, former chief minister of Bihar and member of Parliament, the commission was formed to: (1) Determine the criteria for defining 'socially and educationally backward classes', (2) Recommend steps to be taken for the advancement of socially and educationally backward classes, and (3) Examine the desirability of making provisions for reserving appointments/posts in favour of such backward classes of citizens.

In 1980, the Mandal Commission submitted its report—it applied eleven relative indicators, grouped into three broad heads (social,[23] educational[24] and economic[25]) to ascertain which classes could be treated as socially and economically backward. The commission found 3743 socially and economically backward castes via these parameters—a figure 50 per cent higher than that arrived at by the Kalelkar Commission. From the caste figures based on the census of 1931—the last time a caste census had been conducted in India—as well as the population census of 1971, the Mandal Commission inferred that OBCs (comprising the 3743 castes mentioned earlier) constituted about 52 per cent of the population of India.

Since there already was a 22.5 per cent reservation for SC/ST candidates, introducing 52 per cent reservations for OBCs (in line with their population) would contravene the Supreme Court's decision in *Balaji* and other cases. So, the commission decided to provide for a 27 per cent reservation for OBC candidates, so that the overall ceiling of 50 per cent would not be breached. This quota was to be applicable to the civil services,

---

23 The social indicators relied upon included the following castes/classes: (i) those that were considered socially backward by others, (ii) those that primarily depended upon manual labour for their livelihood, (iii) those where at least 25 per cent of the females and 10 per cent of the males above the state average got married at an age below seventeen years in rural areas and at least 10 per cent of the females and 5 per cent of the males above the state average did so in urban areas, and (iv) those where the participation of females in work was at least 25 per cent above the state average.

24 The educational indicators included castes/classes where: (i) the number of children in the age group of 5–15 years who never attended school was at least 25 per cent above the state average, (ii) the rate of student dropouts in the age group of 5–15 years was at least 25 per cent above the state average, and (iii) the proportion of matriculates was at least 25 per cent below the state average.

25 The economic indicators included castes/classes where: (i) the average value of family assets was at least 25 per cent below the state average, (ii) the number of families living in *kuccha* houses was at least 25 per cent above the state average, (iii) the source of drinking water was beyond 0.5 kilometres for more than 50 per cent of the households, and (iv) the number of households taking consumption loans was at least 25 per cent above the state average.

public sector undertakings, nationalized banks, government-aided firms in the private sector, etc. at the centre and state level. It was also to govern the admission of students to scientific, technical and professional educational institutions funded by the central and state governments. If the recommendations of its report were implemented, the Mandal Commission would have ensured reservations for OBCs in central government establishments for the first time ever.[26]

Several sections of society sharply criticized the Mandal Commission's recommendations and questioned its fundamental methodology of relying on caste figures dating from 1931 to set the OBC population at 52 per cent. Subsequent studies have shown the figure to be much lower.[27]

Many believed that the Mandal Commission report would meet much the same fate as the Kalelkar Commission report. However, in 1990, Prime Minister V.P. Singh decided that his government would implement the Mandal Commission recommendations after ten years of dormancy. This announcement provoked unprecedented violence, protests and rioting, particularly in northern India.[28] Students boycotted classes, blocked traffic, hijacked buses and smashed car windows.[29] One of the most horrific forms of protest was started by Rajiv Goswami, a student of Delhi University, when he doused himself with petrol and

---

26 George H. Gadbois, Jr, *Judges of the Supreme Court of India* (New Delhi: Oxford University Press, 2011), p. 351.

27 Nagarajan, 'Compensatory Discrimination in India', p. 483.

28 V.P. Singh's decision to implement the recommendations of the Mandal Commission resulted in the reduction of his support base and, soon after, the downfall of his government.

29 Jason Morgan-Foster, 'From Hutchins Hall to Hyderabad and Beyond: A Comparative Look at Affirmative Action in Three Jurisdictions', *Washington and Lee Race and Ethnic Ancestry Law Journal*, vol. 9 (2003): p. 73.

attempted self-immolation. This sparked off a series of over 100 self-immolations by students protesting the implementation of the Mandal Commission report. The decision of the V.P. Singh government to legalize the report was a vital reason for its downfall: the reduction of its support base, its premature dissolution and subsequent loss in the general elections that followed.[30]

The Mandal Challenge

Two office memorandums were issued to implement some of the Mandal Commission's recommendations relating to public employment.[31] Read together, the memorandums had the following import: 27 per cent of the civil posts under the Government of India would be reserved for OBCs (including castes/communities common to the Mandal Commission report as well as the respective state government's list of backward classes). Among the backward classes, preference would be given to the poorer sections. If, after giving first preference to poorer sections, there were still vacancies, these could be filled by the others within the backward classes. However, OBCs recruited on the basis of merit would not be adjusted against the 27 per cent quota. Finally, 10 per cent of the vacancies would be reserved

---

30 The 1991 elections were nicknamed the 'Mandal–Mandir' elections, alluding to the two most important electoral issues: (i) reservations for OBCs as per the Mandal Commission recommendations, and (ii) the debate over Babri Masjid at Ayodhya (which right-wing groups claimed was built a few centuries earlier after demolishing a temple at the same site, believed to be the birthplace of Lord Rama).

31 The first office memorandum was issued on 13 August 1990 by the V.P. Singh government. When this government was dissolved, P.V. Narasimha Rao's government issued another one on 25 September 1991, amending the earlier one.

for other economically backward sections uncovered by existing schemes of reservations.[32]

Indra Sawhney, a journalist,[33] filed a public interest litigation (PIL) stating that these memorandums were not constitutionally valid. This PIL was clubbed with several other writ petitions, also challenging the constitutionality of the office memorandums under Article 16 and other provisions of the Constitution. A nine-judge bench of the Supreme Court—which was, at the time, the largest bench ever constituted to hear a reservations case—sat in judgement over the constitutionality of the office memorandums and the constitutional boundaries of India's reservation policy in general.

Off with the 'Creamy Layer'

The judgement was divided. Four of the nine judges delivered a common opinion but each of the others delivered an individual opinion. The majority vote was 6:3 on most questions answered by the court.[34] Recognizing that caste had become the 'cancer cell' of Hindu society and the 'biggest curse' for India,[35] the court emphasized that position in the Hindu caste hierarchy should be used as a criterion to determine if a class could be considered backward. In the case of non-Hindus, the extent of

32 In other words, the memorandums effectively contemplated reservations of 59.5 per cent in Central government posts: 22.5 per cent for SCs/STs (which was already in place), 27 per cent for OBCs, and 10 per cent for other economically backward sections.

33 Manoj Mate, 'Two Paths to Judicial Power: The Basic Structure Doctrine and Public Interest Litigation in Comparative Perspective', *San Diego International Law Journal*, vol. 12 (2010): p. 175.

34 Gadbois, Jr, *Judges of the Supreme Court of India*, p. 351.

35 Justice Kuldip Singh's judgement in *Indra Sawhney*.

backwardness of a community would be assessed on the basis of non-caste factors, such as income level and education. Using an open and pragmatic approach, the court emphasized that it did not aim to perpetuate caste consciousness in India, but it did intend to acknowledge existing social realities rather than sweep them under the carpet.

One of the most serious concerns surrounding the policy of reservations was ensuring that advanced or prosperous members of the backward classes (the 'upper crust') did not exploit a system intended to benefit the destitute and the disadvantaged. In the most well-known portion of the *Indra Sawhney* judgement, the court said that those who formed the 'creamy layer'[36] of OBCs should be excluded from the reservations regime. Any person with a gross annual income above a certain limit[37] should not be allowed to vie for a place in the reserved category. Moreover, as per the 'intergenerational transmission of status'[38] principle, children whose parents held important public positions (for example, in the administrative service, police service or foreign service) should not be permitted to avail of reservations. This was a significantly pertinent principle, especially in India, where most often the socio-economic standing of a child's parents would determine the opportunities available to the child. Excluding those a 'notch above the rest' was the court's method to ensure that the benefits

---

36 The Sattanathan Commission, the first backward classes commission of Tamil Nadu, is credited with using the expression 'creamy layer' for the first time in 1971. Also *see* the Lokur Committee Report of 1965, which recommended 'In the interests of national integration . . . de-scheduling of relatively advanced communities should receive serious and urgent consideration,' and prepared a state-wise list of castes and tribes to be removed from the ambit of beneficiaries.

37 In 1993–94, the limit was set at 1 lakh (100,000) rupees. It was increased to 2.5 (250,000) lakh rupees in 2004 and to 4.5 (450,000) lakh rupees in 2008.

38 Morgan-Foster, 'From Hutchins Hall to Hyderabad and Beyond', p. 73.

of reservation seep to the lowest rungs of backward communities. What specific factors would define the 'creamy layer' though? The court left that to the government's discretion.

The court then found that the 10 per cent quota for economically backward persons (otherwise not entitled to avail of reservation) was unconstitutional. Neither does the Constitution contemplate reservation based solely on economic grounds nor is it aligned with the purpose of reservation—to uplift historically disadvantaged groups, not eradicate poverty in general. It also recognized the 50 per cent ceiling on reservation laid down in the *Balaji* case. Since the 10 per cent reservation for other economically backward persons was invalidated, the remaining reservations contemplated by the memorandums fell within this limit.[39]

The court also disallowed the Mandal Commission's finding that reservations should also apply to promotions, thus restricting its ambit to the appointment stage. The court also said, rightly, with regard to some technical positions (for instance, in the case of pilots, scientists and nuclear technicians), by virtue of the nature of work, appointment should only be based on merit. Lastly, the court ordered that there should be commissions at the central and state level to decide whether a community should be included in or excluded from the 'backward classes' bracket.

The *Indra Sawhney* judgement was criticized for bringing the issue of caste to the fore in Indian politics.[40] Some believe

---

39 As discussed before, the reserved quota amounted to 49.5 per cent of Central government posts—22.5 per cent for SCs/STs and 27 per cent for OBCs.

40 P.P. Rao, 'Right to Equality and the Reservation Policy', *Journal of Indian Law Institute*, vol. 42 (2000): p. 193.

that the decision ushered in a new wave of caste consciousness by virtually equating 'class' with 'caste'. We must, however, give credit to the court for adopting the approach that the first step in addressing a social evil is to acknowledge that it exists.

The Supreme Court's decision was followed by violence and protests in parts of the country, though not as pronounced as that when the V.P. Singh government made its Mandal Commission announcement—this is perhaps because by end-1992, another politico-religious issue had taken centre stage: the Babri Masjid in Ayodhya.[41]

Within three years of the *Indra Sawhney* judgement, the Parliament inserted Article 16(4A)[42] into the Constitution, permitting reservations for SCs and STs to extend to promotions.[43] This was a political tactic and was meant to nullify the portion of the court's judgement that disallowed reservation at the promotion stage.

Extending Mandal to Education

In the years after the *Indra Sawhney* judgement, there were many passionately contested cases on the reservations policy in

---

41 Gadbois, Jr, *Judges of the Supreme Court of India*, p. 351.

42 Article 16(4A) of the Constitution reads: 'Nothing in this article shall prevent the State from making any provision for reservation in matters of promotion, with consequential seniority, to any class or classes of posts in the services under the State in favour of the Scheduled Castes and the Scheduled Tribes which, in the opinion of the State, are not adequately represented in the services under the State.' (Article 16(4A) was amended in 2001. The provision reproduced here reflects the 2001 amendment).

43 The validity of Article 16(4A) of the Constitution was upheld in *Ashok Kumar Gupta v. State of Uttar Pradesh* ((1997) 5 SCC 201).

higher education.[44] Though the controversy over the Mandal Commission recommendations slowly died down, the United Progressive Alliance (UPA) government[45] reignited it in 2006 when it passed the Central Educational Institutions (Reservation in Admission) Act (the CEI Act). This act implemented the report's other recommendations, via which 27 per cent of the seats in all government-funded institutions would be reserved for OBCs. Almost immediately after, a writ petition was filed to challenge the constitutionality of the Act; two years later, the Supreme Court delivered its verdict upholding the Act as constitutionally valid.[46]

The court upheld the act's constitutionality and endorsed the 27 per cent OBC quota. However, as asserted in *Indra Sawhney*, the court reiterated that the benefits of such reservation would not be offered to the 'creamy layer' of the backward classes. Thus, the court continued its effort to minimize the dangers associated with a reservation scheme founded primarily on caste.

In 2012, the Supreme Court upheld the extension of the reservation policy to primary educational institutions as well. Section 12(1) of the Right of Children to Free and Compulsory Education Act, 2009—according to which all primary schools (including private unaided institutions) were to reserve 25 per cent of their seats for children belonging to socio-economically backward classes, SCs and STs—was challenged before the Supreme Court. By a majority of 2:1, the court upheld the

---

44 *T.M.A. Pai Foundation v. State of Karnataka* ((2002) 8 SCC 481); *P.A. Inamdar v. State of Maharashtra* (AIR 2005 SC 3226).

45 The Indian National Congress was the single largest party in this coalition government.

46 *Ashoka Kumar Thakur v. Union of India* ((2008) 6 SCC 1).

provision, explaining that reservations fell within the reasonable restrictions contemplated by Article 19(1)(g), which grants the fundamental right to practise any profession, or carry on any trade, occupation or business (including the right to run educational institutions),[47] stating that reservations constituted a reasonable restriction on the right to run educational institutions under Article 19(1)(g). However, even as the Supreme Court validated reservations in primary educational institutions, it exempted minority institutions from the ambit of the reservation policy.[48]

Caste in India: The Road Ahead

In 2011, under pressure from coalition as well as opposition parties, the UPA government decided to conduct a 'caste census' in India. This was the first caste census since the one under British rule in 1931. There was widespread debate about whether a caste census should be conducted. The decision to count caste figures in India is justified, as no quota should be allowed to operate in a data vacuum. In 1979, the Mandal Commission used the 1931 census to calculate the number of OBCs in India; even today, that data from eighty years ago is the only empirical data based on which we make reservations. There is uncertainty about the exact proportion of OBCs in India; figures ranging from 38

---

47 Article 19(1)(g) of the Constitution guarantees the right to practise any profession, or to carry on any occupation, trade or business subject to: (i) the state's right to make any law in the interests of the general public, (ii) reasonable restrictions on the exercise of the right, and (iii) the state's right to make any law relating to the professional or technical qualifications required to practise any profession, or carry on any occupation, trade or business, or the carrying on by the state of any trade, business, industry or service to the complete or partial exclusion of its citizens.

48 *Association of Unaided Private Schools of Rajasthan v Union of India & Anr.* ((2012) 4 SCALE 272).

per cent to 52 per cent of the population have done the rounds in the last few years.[49] No country can put job and education quotas in place for an underprivileged segment of the population and then bury its head in the sand about the boundaries along which those entitlements are drawn. Apprehensive that caste figures will be inflated, the Union Cabinet, on 9 September 2010, decided to delink the regular population census from the caste census.[50] This is an unhappy situation—not only is there the additional cost, what's more, caste figures are not meaningful or relevant when isolated from the information collected in a regular population census. We need a complete picture of India's caste dilemma before we can seriously think of ways to eradicate it.

Clearly, India's discourse on reservations hinges not on whether it should exist, but on who should benefit from it.[51] At some stage, however, policymakers will have to confront the larger question—how and when can reservations be phased out?

---

49 A survey conducted by the National Sample Survey Organization mentioned the proportion of OBCs to be 36 per cent in 1999–2000 and 40.94 per cent in 2004–05. The Mandal Commission report, published in 1980, estimated OBCs to constitute 52 per cent of the population.

50 *See* Press Information Bureau, Ministry of Home Affairs, Government of India, 'Enumeration of Castes other than Scheduled Castes and Scheduled Tribes', press release, 9 September 2010, http://pib.nic.in/newsite/erelease.aspx?relid=65632 (accessed 20 May 2013).

51 Vanita Goela, 'A Proposed Transjudicial Approach to s. 15(2) Charter Adjudication', *The Dalhousie Law Journal*, vol. 32 (2009): p. 109.

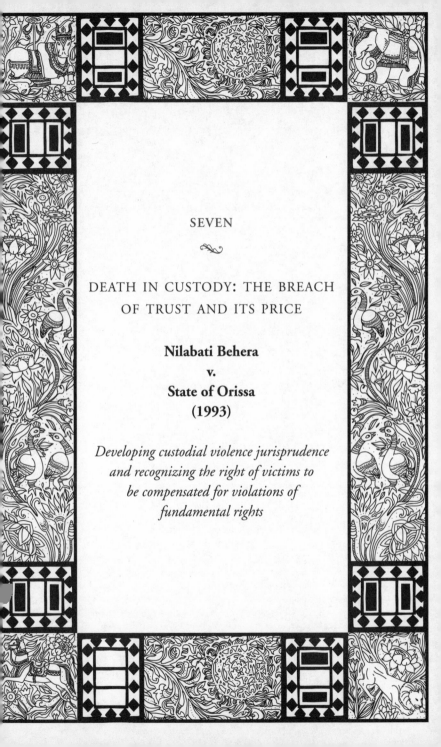

SEVEN

DEATH IN CUSTODY: THE BREACH
OF TRUST AND ITS PRICE

Nilabati Behera
v.
State of Orissa
(1993)

Developing custodial violence jurisprudence
and recognizing the right of victims to
be compensated for violations of
fundamental rights

AFTER HAVING EXPANDED the right to life to include the right to compensation for a breach of this right almost eighty years ago, the Supreme Court has continuously reinforced this jurisprudence. The state has yet to meaningfully formalize a response befitting its citizens living in a democracy.

Introduction

One of the most dangerous cocktails in a democracy is when those who are meant to enforce the law take the law into their own hands. Every week in India, several citizens—usually the poor and those from the weaker sections of society—are killed in police custody. According to the Asian Centre for Human Rights, as many as 1504 custodial deaths were reported to the National Human Rights Commission[1] from April 2001 to March 2010.[2] Most of these deaths occured within forty-eight hours of the victims being taken into police custody. Other reports suggest that there were over a thousand custodial deaths in 2008–09 alone.[3] Let us not forget that these numbers do not reflect a

---

1 An autonomous statutory body established under the Protection of Human Rights Act, 1993 which performs various functions to safeguard human rights in India.

2 Asian Centre for Human Rights, 'Torture in India 2011', November 2011, http://www.achrweb.org/reports/india/torture2011.pdf (accessed 3 January 2013).

3 Pratap Bhanu Mehta, 'The tortured bill', *Indian Express*, 1 September 2010, http://m.indianexpress.com/news/%22the-tortured-bill%22/675580/ (accessed 3 January 2013).

large number of custodial deaths that go unreported in India every year. The most disturbing aspect of custodial violence is that it strikes at the very root of the rule of law in a democracy and shatters the faith of the citizens in the criminal justice system.

If a person is unlawfully detained by the police, the Constitution allows redressal by the filing of a habeas corpus petition under Article 32[4] or 226.[5] Habeas corpus (in Latin, literally '[we command that] you shall have the body') is one of the oldest writ remedies, recognized by courts for centuries. Traditionally, its sole purpose is to have any person under arrest brought to court. Now, if the person has been unlawfully detained, the court can order his release. But what if the remedy loses its meaning even before the court gets to decide the case? What if the person cannot be presented to the court because he has died while in police custody? Prior to the compensatory case law of the Supreme Court, a writ petition in such a case would become meaningless. The only option left to the petitioner would be to file a civil suit for damages against the state for wrongful confinement and a criminal complaint in case of death of the person in custody. Both proceedings would, more often than not, reach a logical conclusion in well over a decade.

Over time, the Supreme Court evolved the remedy of providing compensation to such people, rather than leaving them empty-handed and burdened with the prospect of long-drawn-

---

4   Under Article 32 of the Constitution, the Supreme Court is empowered to issue the writ of habeas corpus.

5   Under Article 226 of the Constitution, high courts in India are empowered to issue the writ of habeas corpus.

out legal proceedings.[6] This 'compensatory jurisprudence' is an example of the Supreme Court's judicial creativity, since granting compensation is not an express part of the relevant provisions of the Constitution.

The Indian Constitution does not expressly mandate the granting of compensation for unlawful detention or custodial death. However, this right is mentioned in several international human rights instruments, including the International Covenant on Civil and Political Rights, 1966 (the ICCPR), one of the most significant global charters on human rights. Article 9(5) of the ICCPR states: '[a]nyone who has been the victim of unlawful arrest or detention shall have an enforceable right to compensation.' In 1979, India acceded to the ICCPR but with a 'reservation'[7] over this provision:

> With reference to Article 9 of the International Covenant on Civil and Political Rights, the Government of the Republic of India takes the position that . . . under the Indian legal system, there is no enforceable right to compensation for persons claiming to be victims of unlawful arrest or detention against the State.[8]

The Constitution of India did recognize that both illegal detention and custodial torture deny the fundamental 'right to

---

6 *See* J.L. Kaul and Anju Vali Tikoo, 'Revisiting Award of Compensation for Violation of Fundamental Human Rights: An Analysis of Indian Supreme Court Decisions', www.ailtc.org/downloads/Revisiting_Award_of_Compensation.doc (accessed 3 October 2012).

7 A reservation is a unilateral statement made by a state when accepting a treaty, in which it declares that it will exclude or modify the legal effect of certain provisions of the treaty in their application to that state.

8 Justice G. Yethirajulu, 'Article 32 and the Remedy of Compensation', (2004) 7 SCC (J) 49.

life', but in the early decades after India's independence, courts did only the following:[9]

1. If the complaint pertained to illegal detention, the court ordered that the detained person be set free.

2. If there was evidence of illegal detention or custodial violence, the court directed the concerned government to hold an inquiry and take action against the officers responsible.

3. If the court was not satisfied by the inquiry conducted or action taken by the relevant government department, it ordered another inquiry by an independent agency, usually, the Central Bureau of Investigation (CBI).

Bhagalpur Blindings and *Rudul Sah*: From Recognizing the Right to Compensation to Enforcing It

The Supreme Court recognized the right to seek compensation via a habeas corpus petition for the first time in the *Khatri v. State of Bihar* cases, better known as the 'Bhagalpur blinding' cases. In 1979–80, police officials at Bhagalpur Central Jail in Bihar blinded thirty-one undertrial prisoners by pouring acid into their eyes. Coming down heavily on the state authorities in a series of cases involving these blindings, the Supreme Court said that it should prepare to 'forge new tools and devise new remedies'[10] for the meaningful enforcement of the right to life, else the right would be reduced to a 'mere rope of sand'.[11] The court conceptualized a right to grant monetary compensation

---

9   *Sube Singh v. State of Haryana* (AIR 2006 SC 1117).

10 *Khatri v. State of Bihar* (AIR 1981 SC 928).

11 *Khatri v. State of Bihar* (AIR1981 SC 1068).

for infringements of the right to life under the Constitution. However, since the investigation of the accused police officers was pending, it did not actually grant any compensation to the victims.[12] In 1980, the CBI Special Magistrate held three officers guilty for the custodial deaths of the undertrials. When the officers appealed to the district and sessions judge and were acquitted, the CBI appealed to the Patna High Court, which upheld the conviction of two of the three accused police officers in the Bhagalpur blindings case.[13]

It took another equally disturbing scenario to prompt the Supreme Court to award compensation for the violation of fundamental rights for the first time in *Rudul Sah v. State of Bihar*[14] (*Rudul Sah*). In 1968, Rudul Sah was acquitted of a murder charge by a criminal court in Muzaffarpur, Bihar, yet he languished in jail for fourteen years after that. In 1982, he filed a habeas corpus petition in the Supreme Court seeking his release from unlawful custody. He was finally released after he filed the writ but before the date of the Supreme Court hearing. Though Sah was released, the court continued to hear the matter and demanded an explanation for his prolonged incarceration. Bihar police authorities offered flimsy grounds (principally, that the petitioner was of unsound mind) for keeping Sah in jail. Disapproving strongly of the state's approach to the case, the Supreme Court questioned 'whether it took fourteen years to

---

12 Paramjit S. Jaswal, 'Public Accountability for Violation of Human Rights and Judicial Activism in India: Some Observations', (2002) 3 SCC (J) 6.

13 'Bhagalpur blinding case: HC upholds conviction of two accused', *Times of India* (3 May 2011), http://articles.timesofindia.indiatimes.com/2011-05-03/patna/29498702_1_chargesheet-justice-dharnidhar-jha-cbi-court (accessed 5 January 2013).

14 AIR 1983 SC 1086.

set right his mental imbalance'.[15] The court also observed that the claim of the petitioner's insanity was 'an afterthought' and 'exaggerated out of proportion' and, if at all he were insane at some stage, the insanity 'must have supervened as a consequence of his unlawful detention in jail',[16] as '[a] sense of helplessness and frustration can create despondency and persistent despondency can lead to a kind of mental imbalance'.[17]

A refusal to grant Sah compensation would have been be a grave injustice, tantamount to mere lip service to the right to personal liberty under Article 21 of the Constitution. The court recognized this and awarded Sah compensation of 30,000 rupees as a 'palliative' for the illegalities committed by the state. The judgement had a few caveats though. First, the court observed that the petitioner would have been relegated to filing a civil suit and instituting criminal proceedings if his claim had been 'factually controversial'. Second, it stated that seeking an award of compensation under Article 32 of the Constitution could not be used as a substitute for filing a regular money claim in a civil court; the court's order granting compensation was attributable to the serious inequities that would have denied immediate compensation to Sah. Finally, the court clarified that the award of compensation would not bar Sah from also invoking the remedy of a civil suit. Clearly, the court's decision signified that the ordinary remedy to seek damages from the state is through ordinary civil (tortious) law. The compensation provided to Sah was an exception—it was an attempt to undo the injustice done unto an innocent man.

---

15 *Rudul Sah*, p. 511 .
16 Ibid., p. 512.
17 Ibid.

The court's decision in *Rudul Sah* has been critiqued because it awarded compensation so meagre that it would barely suffice to assist the victim in pursuing his rights through the 'labyrinthine legal system',[18] let alone balm the wounds of his unlawful incarceration. Since it was the first time that compensation was awarded for violation of fundamental rights, the Supreme Court understandably did not grant a large sum to Sah. However, it did introduce the vitally important element of compensation in constitutional proceedings before the Supreme Court and high courts. Such an expansive interpretation of Article 21 imposed a duty on the state to protect human liberty,[19] or pay a tangible monetary compensation if it failed to do so.

How the Right to Compensation Was Crystallized

In the decade following *Rudul Sah*, the Supreme Court awarded small sums of compensation as redress for the violation of the right to life under the Constitution. In *Bhim Singh v. State of Jammu and Kashmir*,[20] Bhim Singh, a member of the Legislative Assembly of Jammu and Kashmir, was unlawfully arrested to prevent him from attending an Assembly session. His wife filed a petition before the Supreme Court seeking his release. Though Bhim Singh was released before the hearing, the court observed that in such cases of illegal detention, the illegality could not

---

18 Upendra Baxi, 'A Perspective from India', www.uu.nl/faculty/leg/nl/organisatie/departementen/departementenrechtsgeleerdheid/organisatie/onderdelen/studieeninformatiecentrummensenrechten/publicaties/simspecials/12/Documents/12-08.pdf (accessed 30 September 2012).

19 A. Raghunadha Reddy, 'Reparation of the Wrong: Problems and Perspectives (An Evaluation on the Compensation for the Breach of Fundamental Rights)', *NALSAR Law Review*, vol. 2 (2004–2005): p. 71.

20 AIR 1986 SC 494.

be 'washed away or wished away' merely by freeing the person. Since it had the power to award monetary compensation, the court ordered the state to pay Bhim Singh the suitable sum of 50,000 rupees. The court did not elaborate how the amount of compensation was calculated.

In another case,[21] the Delhi Police colluded with a landlord who wanted to unlawfully evict two female tenants. The two women were beaten up and the nine-year-old son of one of them died due to police brutality. The court ordered compensation of 75,000 rupees to be paid to the mother for the murder of her child.

In another blatant violation of fundamental rights, police authorities in Sholapur, Maharashtra paraded an undertrial prisoner (accused of murder) through the streets, his hands cuffed and his arms tied together.[22] The Supreme Court ordered the state of Maharashtra to pay compensation for this unpardonable act of humiliation, but set the amount at merely 10,000 rupees.

Finally, it was a case involving the high-handedness of Orissa police officials that provided the Supreme Court an opportunity to systematically analyse the right to seek compensation for infractions of Article 21.[23] In *Nilabati Behera v. State of Orissa*[24] (*Nilabati Behera*), the court took a simple letter sent by Nilabati Behera to the Supreme Court—stating that her twenty-two-year-old son Suman Behera had died in police custody—and converted it into a writ petition.[25]

---

21 *Saheli v. Commissioner of Police, Delhi Police Headquarters* (AIR 1990 SC 513).

22 *State of Maharashtra v. Ravikant Patil* ((1991) 2 SCC 373).

23 Article 21 of the Constitution reads: '[n]o person shall be deprived of his life or personal liberty except according to procedure established by law.'

24 AIR 1993 SC 1960.

25 This was an instance of the court taking *suo motu* action encompassing action

The Orissa police had arrested Suman for allegedly committing a theft. Barely a day after he was taken into custody, his dead body was found near a railway track. The lacerations on his body suggested that he had died an unnatural death. His mother sought compensation, claiming that the police had violated her son's right to life under Article 21. Countering that Suman had escaped from police custody and was run over by a passing train, the police and the state disclaimed responsibility for his death. Interestingly, the Additional Solicitor-General appearing for the state did not dispute the state's liability to pay compensation if it were established that Suman actually died in police custody. A doctor deposed before the court that all of Suman's injuries were caused by blunt objects and could have been the result of lathi blows. The medical evidence dismissed the possibility of injury in a train accident.

The court distinguished between the 'public law'[26] remedy of compensation for the violation of fundamental rights from ordinary remedies via private law proceedings like civil suits. The court also took into account 'sovereign immunity' on account of which the state and its officers are immune from legal proceedings relating to any act done in the exercise of the state's 'sovereign functions'.[27] In *Nilabati Behera*, the court asserted that the sovereign immunity defence would not be available in public

---

undertaken by a judge on his/her own accord, without request by either party to the action before the court.

26 The law governing the relationship between individuals and the state.

27 The applicability of this doctrine, imported from English law, to tort claims in India, was acknowledged by the Supreme Court in the much-criticized decision of *Kasturi Lal v. State of U.P.* (AIR 1965 SC 1039).

law proceedings under Article 32[28] or 226[29] of the Constitution, though it could apply to proceedings in private law involving torts committed by the state.

The court also watered down the caveats it had imposed in *Rudul Sah* on awarding compensation for violation of the right to life, stating that it was an 'acknowledged remedy for enforcement and protection' of fundamental rights. It stressed that it would be highly inequitable and unjust to expect a socio-economically disadvantaged person—who did not possess the wherewithal for enforcement of his rights in tort law—to pursue ordinary civil proceedings. It awarded a compensation of 1.5 lakh (150,000) rupees to Nilabati Behera and ordered the state of Orissa to initiate criminal proceedings against those who killed her son.

Thus, for the very first time, the Supreme Court drew the distinction between compensation as a remedy in public law and private law proceedings.[30] Until the *Nilabati Behera* judgement, compensation was granted on an ad hoc basis, without any structured formulation. The Supreme Court crystallized this remedy into a rule of law through its verdict in 1993.

Eleven Commandments against Custodial Violence

Ironically, in spite of the emphatic decisions of the Supreme Court strongly condemning all forms of custodial violence, cases of custodial deaths actually increased in the 1980s. In August

---

28 Article 32 of the Indian Constitution guarantees the right to move the Supreme Court for the enforcement of fundamental rights.

29 Article 226 of the Indian Constitution deals with the right to move high courts for the enforcement of fundamental rights or any other legal rights.

30 Kaul and Tikoo, 'Revisiting Award of Compensation for Violation of Fundamental Human Rights', www.ailtc.org/downloads/Revisiting_Award_of_Compensation.doc.

1986, D.K. Basu, lawyer and executive chairman of an NGO that provided legal aid services in West Bengal and later appointed a judge of the Calcutta High Court, wrote to the Chief Justice of India to draw his attention to several news articles reporting deaths in police custody. In Basu's words, he wanted to 'persuade the Chief Justice that violence, death, rape, assault and injuries in custody have become the rule of the government in police administration'.[31] He urged that 'the court should . . . prescribe some strong modalities, for the manner in which India's citizens should be treated in police custody'.[32] Treating Basu's letter as a writ petition, the Supreme Court issued notices to all state governments in India[33]—since the question of custodial death had assumed significance on a national scale. It also asked the Law Commission of India to suggest ways to tackle the disturbing situation.

The court lamented the fact that cases of custodial torture and death were on the rise, in spite of constitutional safeguards and legislative protection available to those in police custody. It commented that '[i]f the functionaries of the Government become law breakers, it is bound to breed contempt for law and would encourage lawlessness.'[34] It also observed that India's reservation to the ICCPR (on the absence of an enforceable right to compensation) had lost relevance, since the right to claim compensation had been judicially evolved in several cases.

---

31 'A Life Devoted to Providing Access to India's Legal System and Averting Abuses in Police Custody: Interview with D.K. Basu', *Human Rights Solidarity Journal*, vol. 16, no. 2 (2006), http://www.hrsolidarity.net/mainfile.php/2006vol16no02/2492/ (accessed 13 February 2013).

32 Ibid.

33 Another instance of the Supreme Court taking *suo motu* action.

34 *D.K. Basu v. State of West Bengal* (AIR 1997 SC 610).

Acting pragmatically, the court declared that punishing the offender in cases of custodial death may not always be enough. It analysed case law in nations like Ireland and New Zealand to firmly establish an enforceable right to compensation against the state in case of violation of fundamental rights. Awarding compensation was perhaps the only effective remedy available in such cases. The court also reiterated the distinction between public law remedies and private law remedies, as discussed in *Nilabati Behera*.

Then, the court listed eleven mandatory requirements for police authorities across India (*see* Appendix I on page 157). These included conducting regular medical examinations of the person in custody, the right to inform a friend or relative of the arrest, access to a lawyer during interrogation, and so on. Not only did the court order that these requirements be circulated to all police stations in India, it also innovatively suggested that they be broadcast on All India Radio and telecast on Doordarshan.

However, there was one very disappointing aspect of the judgement. The Supreme Court's 'eleven commandments' did not include the right to obtain compensation from the state in all cases of custodial violence. That would have increased awareness of the enforceable right to compensation among citizens, given that the court's guidelines would receive greater publicity and prominence in daily life than the court's judgement. Even ten years after the judgement, Basu regretted this aspect in an interview:

> One addition has not been made [to the guidelines of the Supreme Court] that is absolutely necessary: a court should pass an order awarding compensation in cases of death, rape or any kind of injury to anyone while in custody as compensation is

presently not prescribed in the guidelines given by the Supreme Court.[35]

How the Law Evolved after the Basu Judgement

Gradually, the Supreme Court and high courts expanded the people's right to claim compensation from the state in cases besides that of custodial death. In a deplorable incident where a minor committed suicide after being raped in police custody, the Gujarat High Court awarded interim compensation of 1.5 lakh (150,000) rupees even though a departmental inquiry was pending.[36] In another case where a Bangladeshi national was gang-raped by railway employees, the Supreme Court extended the right to seek compensation to foreign nationals—all persons enjoy the right to life under Article 21.[37]

The Delhi High Court has been quite progressive in awarding compensation for the negligence of state authorities. In *Shakuntala v. Govt. of NCT of Delhi*,[38] the petitioner's husband, a fruit vendor and the family's sole breadwinner, was fatally injured in a fight between two stray bulls on a Delhi street. He died soon thereafter. His wife claimed that the Municipal Corporation of Delhi had failed miserably in its duty to ensure that stray

---

35 A Life Devoted to Providing Access to India's Legal System', http://www.hrsolidarity. net/mainfile.php/2006vol16no02/2492/.

36 *Bachiben Naranbha v. State of Gujarat* ((2007) 3 GLR 1918) (Gujarat High Court).

37 *Chairman, Railway Board v. Chandrima Das* (AIR 2000 SC 988); in a case that received widespread publicity, the Delhi High Court awarded compensation to Bangladeshi national Tasleema Nasreen on account of her son suffering mental torture at the hands of the police—*Tasleema v. State (NCT of Delhi)* ((2009) ILR 6 Delhi 486) (Delhi High Court).

38 2010 ACJ 1 (Delhi High Court).

animals do not roam the streets and sought compensation for her husband's death. The court held:

> The relief of compensation under public law, for injuries caused on account of negligent action, or inaction or indifference of public functionaries or for the violation of fundamental rights is a part of the evolving public law jurisprudence in India . . . Compensation under public law must not be merely seen as the monetary equivalent for compensating towards the injury caused, but also understood in the context of the failure of the State or state agency, to protect the valuable rights of the citizens, particularly of the marginalized and the disempowered.[39]

That the court awarded a respectable sum of 10 lakh (1 million) rupees to the petitioner as compensation was not the only important aspect of this judgement. What was equally, if not more, important was that it extended the right to seek compensation to cases where public functionaries and local bodies had been negligent. Thus, it did away with the cloak of 'sovereign immunity' previously enjoyed by public officials as a defence against acts of negligence. A police officer too has benefited from the enforceable right to compensation. In *Shyama Devi v. National Capital Territory of Delhi*,[40] a police constable died a freakish death due to gross negligence—a rocket belonging to the army was not defused. Holding that the right to life is non-negotiable, the court ordered the state to pay a

---

39 2010 ACJ 1 (Delhi High Court).
40 AIR 1999 Del 264 (Delhi High Court).

compensation of 3.5 lakh (350,000) rupees to the constable's family. This opened the door to the fact that officers of the state could themselves move court and claim compensation for violation of their fundamental rights.

What Price Is the Right Price?

Ever since the Supreme Court first awarded compensation in *Rudul Sah*, the basis for calculating the quantum of compensation has been a vexed legal issue. After all, granting inadequate or paltry sums of money would only perpetuate the injustice. *Lakshmana Naidu v. State of Tamil Nadu*[41] (*Lakshmana Naidu*) provides an interesting example of how courts determine the quantum of compensation. The petitioners claimed compensation of 5 lakh (500,000) rupees for each of the three persons who died at the hands of forest officials.[42] However, using the 'multiplier method',[43] the court found that the families of the three persons were entitled to over 7 lakh (700,000) rupees each. And yet, surprisingly, the court ruled: 'As the petitioners themselves . . . claimed only 5 lakh rupees as compensation in each of the writ petitions . . . ends of justice would be met if

---

41   (2006) 3 MLJ 764 (Madras High Court).

42   Local policemen asked three villagers to abet them in certain illegal activities. When they refused, the policemen threatened them that they would be accused of sandalwood theft. One day, the three villagers went out to run some errands, but did not return. Their bodies were later found in the forest, all of them burnt. It came to light that the three policemen had interrogated and beaten up the three men, one of whom died in the process. With the help of forest officials, the policemen burnt the corpse of the dead man, then poisoned the other two and burnt their bodies as well.

43   In the multiplier method, the loss of dependency coupled with several other factors—such as the number of dependents, age, nature of profession and future prospects of the deceased—are considered to determine the quantum of damages to be awarded by the court to the deceased.

the respondent State is directed to pay a sum of 5 lakh rupees to the petitioners.'[44]

In this case, the court behaved regressively by restricting the compensation to the claimed amount despite acknowledging that the petitioners were entitled to a larger amount. The court's approach went against the very philosophy of the court itself that it should mould remedies to ensure complete justice in exercise of its writ jurisdiction.[45] By reducing the compensation granted to the amount claimed, the court would only encourage petitioners to make extravagant compensation claims to somehow ensure that the amount calculated by the court did not exceed the amount claimed as compensation. The courts should not hesitate in awarding compensation exceeding the claim if they find that the case circumstances justify the claim.

There is no consistency yet in calculating the compensation amount to be granted for violation of the right to life. Although the enforceable right to compensation has been established beyond all doubt in India, the compensation amount has been a matter of debate; different benches across the Supreme Court and the various high courts have applied different approaches and methodologies. The accompanying table shows the compensation awarded by courts in some cases since *Rudul Sah*. From as little as 10,000 rupees awarded by the Supreme Court in 1991 in a case of insult to individual dignity to as much as

---

44 *Lakshmana Naidu* at para. 15.

45 *See* also *Abdul Rashid Beigh v. State of Jammu and Kashmir* (2004 Cr.L.J. 1706), where, regrettably, the Jammu and Kashmir High Court awarded 2 lakh (200,000) rupees as compensation for the unlawful arrest of a cameraman working with the Department of South Asian Studies, University of Kashmir—a figure less than half of the 5-lakh-rupee (500,000-rupee) amount recommended by the state human rights commission.

10 lakh (1 million) rupees awarded by the Calcutta High Court in 2000 to a victim of rape by railway employees, the calculation of compensation amounts has been erratic and inconsistent. It is extremely important to develop a unified jurisprudence to determine the quantum of compensation for infringements on the right to life, otherwise there is a risk that victims and their families might start to consider a compensation case as a lottery.

Compensation with Caution

Despite the dozens of cases that have acknowledged the right to award compensation in public law proceedings, courts still tread cautiously in cases where petitioners seek compensation for the violation of fundamental rights. Firstly, compensation can only be awarded for violation of the right to life under Article 21—no other fundamental right.[46] Moreover, not every violation of the right to life justifies compensation—only violations that shock the court's conscience.[47] Finally, even when the state seriously violates the right to life, compensation can be denied if the petitioner falsifies or exaggerates claims.[48]

When the Supreme Court, in the case of *Sube Singh v. State of Haryana,*[49] heard an unsubstantiated claim of illegal detention and torture by the police of a man instead of his son (the accused), despite the fact that the father denied all knowledge of his son's whereabouts, the Supreme Court took the opportunity to define

---

46 *Hindustan Paper Corporation Ltd. v. Ananta Bhattacharjee* ((2004) 6 SCC 213); *see* also *Santhoshima Parboiled Modern Rice v. District Collector* (2010 (5) ALD 310) (Andhra Pradesh High Court).

47 *M.C. Mehta v. Union of India* (AIR 1987 SC 1086).

48   *Dhananjay Sharma v. State of Haryana* (AIR 1995 SC 1795).

49 AIR 2006 SC 1117.

the range of cases where compensation would be awarded on an allegation of custodial torture.[50] It specified three questions that any court must pose when debating whether or not to grant compensation for the violation of fundamental rights:[51]

1. Was the violation of the right to life patent and incontrovertible?
2. Was the violation gross and of a magnitude to shock the court's conscience?
3. Did the custodial torture allegedly result in death or was the custodial torture supported by a medical report or visible marks or scars or disability?

That the Supreme Court is cautious in awarding compensation is understandable—if it does not restrict cases involving grant of compensation for the violation of fundamental rights, it is possible that people, parties or litigants may attempt to enforce private law actions in the garb of public law actions, since courts decide the latter more swiftly.

The court refused to award compensation, citing that there existed a serious dispute as to factum of harassment by police, in a case that received widespread press coverage involving the alleged molestation (though not in custody) by a police officer of a minor girl, Ruchika Girhotra, who later committed suicide.[52] In this case, Ruchika's brother stated that the police systematically framed him in a car theft—to pressurize his family to drop charges against the accused officer—and claimed compensation for the harassment.

---

50 Ibid.
51 Ibid.
52 *S.P.S. Rathore v. State of Haryana* ((2005) 10 SCC 1).

The How and How Much of Compensation: Why We Need a Law

The Constitution of India does not grant an enforceable right to compensation; yet, the courts have recognized it and awarded it. This reflects how seriously the judiciary wants to respond to the aspirations of the people and become a sentinel of human rights in India.[53] Unfortunately, the seriousness of the judgements has not sufficiently influenced the attitude of the government officials and police authorities. What's more, there is still no definite clarity on the amount of compensation awarded by courts—there is still a preponderant element of chance or 'waywardness'[54] to it. Since no uniform basis has been formulated for the grant of compensation in over three decades, the amounts of compensation awarded have fluctuated from a few thousand rupees in some cases to lakhs of rupees in others. This uncertainty does not help matters.

The National Commission to Review the Working of the Constitution, set up by the Atal Behari Vajpayee government in 2000, recommended an amendment to Article 21 to include 'an enforceable right to compensation' for every person illegally deprived of his right to life or liberty.[55] Amending the right to life may be useful to universalize the right to seek compensation, but the need of the hour also is to enact legislation to set out the

---

53 *See* Reddy, 'Reparation of the Wrong', p. 71.

54 *See* Baxi, 'A Perspective from India', www.uu.nl/faculty/leg/nl/organisatie/ departementen/departementrechtsgeleerdheid/organisatie/onderdelen/ studieeninformatiecentrummensenrechten/publicaties/simspecials/12/ Documents/12-08.pdf.

55 Ministry of Law, Justice and Company Affairs, 'Report of the National Commission to Review the Working of the Constitution', vol. I, chapter 3 (2002), para. 310, http://lawmin.nic.in/ncrwc/finalreport/volume1.htm (accessed 12 February 2013).

parameters on which compensation should be granted. It is well worth enacting a separate law to put in place a formal structure to grant monetary compensation in case of violations of the right to life and personal liberty. The law should also focus on providing compensation swifter than, or at least as swiftly as, a writ remedy under Article 32 of the Constitution. If it does not do so, the legislation will become counterproductive and act to the detriment of the citizens.

APPENDIX I

**Guidelines on Arrest and Detention Issued by the
Supreme Court in *D.K. Basu v. State of West Bengal*:[56]
The 'Eleven Commandments'**

1. The police personnel carrying out the arrest and handling the interrogation of the arrestee should bear accurate, visible and clear identification and name tags with their designations. The particulars of all such police personnel who handle interrogation of the arrestee must be recorded in a register.

2. The police officer carrying out the arrest of the arrestee shall prepare a memo of arrest at the time of arrest and such memo shall be attested by at least one witness, who may be either a member of the family of the arrestee or a respectable person of the locality from where the arrest is made. It shall also be countersigned by the arrestee and shall contain the time and date of arrest.

3. A person who has been arrested or detained and is being held in custody at a police station or interrogation centre or other lock-up, shall be entitled to have one friend or relative or other person known to him [or her] or having interest in his welfare being informed, as soon as practicable, that he has been arrested and is being detained at the particular place, unless the attesting witness of the memo of arrest is himself such a friend or a relative of the arrestee.

4. The time, place of arrest and venue of custody of an arrestee must be notified by the police where the next friend or relative of the arrestee lives outside the district or town through the legal aid organization in the district, and the police station of

---

56 AIR 1997 SC 610.

the area concerned, telegraphically, within a period of eight to twelve hours after the arrest.

5. The person arrested must be made aware of this right to have someone informed of his arrest or detention as soon as he is put under arrest or detained.

6. An entry must be made in the diary at the place of detention regarding the arrest of the person which shall also disclose the name of the next friend of the person who has been informed of the arrest and the names and particulars of the police officials in whose custody the arrestee is.

7. The arrestee should, where he so requests, be also examined at the time of his arrest and major and minor injuries, if any present on his/her body, must be recorded at that time. The inspection memo must be signed both by the arrestee and the police officer effecting the arrest and its copy provided to the arrestee.

8. The arrestee should be subjected to medical examination by a trained doctor every forty-eight hours during his detention in custody by a doctor on the panel of approved doctors appointed by Director, Health Services, of the concerned State or Union Territory. The Director, Health Services, should prepare such a penal for all tehsils and districts as well.

9. Copies of all the documents, including the memo of arrest referred to above, should be sent to the *illaqa* magistrate for his record.

10. The arrestee may be permitted to meet his lawyer during interrogation, though not throughout the interrogation.

11. A police control room should be provided at all district and state headquarters, where information regarding the arrest and the place of custody of the arrestee shall be communicated by the officer causing the arrest, within twelve hours of effecting the arrest and at the police control room it should be displayed on a conspicuous notice board.

APPENDIX II

Compensation(s) Granted by Courts for Violation of the Right to Life under Article 21 of the Constitution

Case	Year	Court	Illegality Committed by the State	Compensation Granted (Amount in INR)
Rudul Sah	1983	Supreme Court	Wrongful confinement (for over 14 years despite acquittal)	30,000
Sebastian Hongray v. Union of India ((1984) 3 SCC 82)	1983	Supreme Court	Custodial death	1,00,000
Bhim Singh v. State of Jammu and Kashmir (AIR 1986 SC 494)	1985	Supreme Court	Wrongful confinement	50,000
Saheli v. Commissioner of Police, Delhi Police Headquarters (AIR 1990 SC 513)	1989	Supreme Court	Death on account of police brutality	75,000
State of Maharashtra v. Ravikant Patil (AIR 1990 SC 513)	1991	Supreme Court	Public humiliation and insult to dignity	10,000
Nilabati Behera	1993	Supreme Court	Custodial death	1,50,000
Charanjit Kaur v. Union of India ((1994) 2 SCC 1)	1994	Supreme Court	Death of an officer of the army under mysterious circumstances	6,00,000
Shyama Devi v. National Capital Territory of Delhi (AIR 1999 Del 264)	1999	Delhi High Court	Death of a police constable on account of negligence by the state	3,50,000
Chairman, Railway Board v. Chandrima Das (AIR 2000 SC 988)	2000	Supreme Court / Calcutta High Court	Rape of a foreign national by railway employees	10,00,000

Case	Year	Court	Illegality Committed by the State	Compensation Granted (Amount in INR)
Abdul Rashid Beigh v. State of Jammu and Kashmir (2004 Cr.L.J. 1706)	2003	Jammu and Kashmir High Court	Disappearance after being taken in police custody	2,00,000
Bachiben Naranbha v. State of Gujarat ((2007) 3 GLR 1918)	2006	Gujarat High Court	Rape and torture of a minor in police custody, resulting in suicide by minor	1,50,000 (interim compensation)*
Lakshmana Naidu v. State of Tamil Nadu ((2006) 3 MLJ)	2006	Madras High Court	Murder of three persons at the hands of forest officials	5,00,000 (each)
Shakuntala v. Govt. of NCT of Delhi (2010 ACJ 1)	2009	Delhi High Court	Death on account of failure to keep the streets free from stray cattle	10,00,000
Tasleema v. State (NCT of Delhi) ((2009) ILR 6 Delhi 486)	2009	Delhi High Court	Abduction and mental harassment of a minor	2,70,000
Prempal v. Commissioner of Police ((2010) ILR 4 Delhi 416)	2010	Delhi High Court	Harassment by the police and wrongful incarceration	5,32,750

* Paid by the state government; however, the judgement specifies that this amount should be recovered from the individual police officers if they are found to be guilty when investigations are completed.

EIGHT

COURTING LIBERTY:
INDEPENDENCE OF THE
JUDICIARY AS ENVISAGED BY
THE CONSTITUTION OF INDIA

**Supreme Court Advocates-on-Record
Association
v.
Union of India
(1993)**

*Settling the power of the Supreme Court of
India to make judicial appointments*

NO DEMOCRACY CAN flourish without an independent judicial system, a system free from fear or favour, a system isolated from the other branches of government. It enhances the prosperity and stability of the social order.[1] Too often, civil society undermines the importance of an independent judiciary while legal professionals overlook it.[2] Today, the activist Indian judiciary adjudicates disputes as diverse as river water distribution between states, the legality of a governor's proclamation of President's rule in a state, and even matters involving allegations of corruption by high-ranking public officials including the Prime Minister and members of Parliament. In fact, in the context of the Indian democracy, citizens disillusioned with the political system often resort to the Supreme Court as their last hope. In such circumstances, it is imperative to safeguard the independence of the judiciary so that it continues to play a proactive role in our democracy.

The Constitution includes several mechanisms, such as the following, to protect the independence of judges of the Supreme Court and high courts:

---

1   M.P. Singh, 'Securing the Independence of the Judiciary: The Indian Experience', *Indiana International and Comparative Law Review*, vol. 10 (2000): p. 245.

2   For instance, in a legal article, the case of *S.P. Gupta v. President of India* (AIR 1982 SC 149) (later discussed as the *First Judges Case*)—which touched on critical issues involving judicial independence—has been described as one that did not have anything 'memorable' about the facts of the case; *see* Parvez Hassan and Azim Azfar, 'Securing Environmental Rights through Public Interest Litigation in South Asia', *Virginia Environmental Law Journal*, vol. 22 (2004): p. 215.

1. Judges can be removed only through a cumbersome 'impeachment motion' in the Parliament and only on grounds of proven misbehaviour or incapacity.[3]
2. The service conditions of judges cannot be altered to their detriment during their terms of office.[4]
3. The Parliament is barred from discussing the conduct of judges except in the case of an impeachment motion.[5]
4. The administrative expenses of courts are charged to the Consolidated Fund[6] of India or of the relevant state, and are not subject to discussion in the Parliament.[7]

However, these provisions alone cannot preserve judicial integrity. The powers to appoint or not appoint, to transfer or not transfer, and to promote or not promote judges are equally important elements that influence the independent standing of the judiciary.[8]

Article 124 of the Constitution says that every judge of the Supreme Court should be appointed by the President[9] after

---

3   The applicable provision for Supreme Court judges is Article 124(4) of the Constitution, whereas Article 217(1)(b) is applicable to high court judges.

4   The applicable provision for Supreme Court judges is Article 125 of the Constitution, whereas Article 221 is applicable to high court judges.

5   Article 121 of the Constitution bars the Parliament from such discussion, whereas Article 211 bars the state legislature from the same.

6   Funds established under Article 266 of the Constitution at the central and state levels.

7   The applicable provision for the Supreme Court is Article 146(3) of the Constitution, whereas Article 229(3) is applicable to high courts.

8   Arun Shourie, *Mrs. Gandhi's Second Reign* (Ghaziabad: Vikas Publishing House, 1984), p. 243.

9   Although the power to appoint judges is formally vested in the President, this power effectively belongs to the executive branch of government since the President acts on the aid and advice of the Council of Ministers (Article 74 of the Constitution).

consulting the Chief Justice of India (CJI) and other judges of the Supreme Court and high courts. As for the judges of the twenty-one high courts in India, Article 217 says that every high court judge should be appointed by the President after consulting with the CJI, the governor of the relevant state and the chief justice of that high court. The President is empowered to transfer a judge from one high court to another after consulting with the CJI.[10] The Constitution also enables the President to appoint 'additional judges' for a maximum of two years to meet a temporary increase in business or work arrears in any high court.[11] These provisions seem fairly clear. However, subsequent developments since the promulgation of the Constitution (political as well as legal) have complicated the way that simple expressions concerning the higher judiciary are interpreted.

Appointment of Judges in Practice

The makers of our Constitution believed that they had done whatever they possibly could to secure the independence of the judiciary.[12] The Constitution was drafted with the hope that the executive and the judiciary would work in unison to ensure that judicial appointments are based on merit. Expressions such as 'consultation' (between the President and the CJI) were deliberately used to ensure that no single authority would wield absolute power.

In the early years of Indian democracy, judicial appointments

---

10 Article 222 of the Constitution.

11 Article 224 of the Constitution.

12 Singh, 'Securing the Independence of the Judiciary', p. 245.

were made according to plan.[13] As a healthy practice, the opinions of the CJI and the chief justice of the appropriate high court were considered as most relevant in making appointments. This changed drastically under the Indira Gandhi-led Congress government of the 1970s, the decade that witnessed sharp conflicts between the political class and the judiciary.[14] In an unprecedented act of supersession which left India stunned, Justice A.N. Ray suddenly became the CJI, bypassing the three senior-most judges of the Supreme Court, Justices J.M. Shelat, K.S. Hegde and A.N. Grover who had earlier pronounced judgements[15] that had not found favour with the Congress government.

Democracy needed rescuing. And here began a bitter struggle for power between the judiciary and the executive. The power to transfer high court judges under the Constitution was meant to be used only in certain exigencies—never to penalize independent judges. During the twenty-one-month long national Emergency between 1975 and 1977, as many as fifty-six high court judges were transferred from their home high court to high courts in other states as punishment for not falling in line with the policies of the Indira Gandhi government.[16] Sixteen of these judges were transferred on one day alone.[17] One of the judges, Justice Sankalchand Sheth—transferred from the Gujarat

---

13 Fali S. Nariman, *Before Memory Fades: An Autobiography* (New Delhi: Hay House, 2010), p. 390.

14 For a detailed discussion of the struggle between the judiciary and the elected government in the 1970s, *see* Chapter One for an analysis of the Supreme Court's decision in *Kesavananda Bharati v. State of Kerala* (AIR 1973 SC 1461).

15 *Kesavananda Bharati v. State of Kerala*, AIR 1973 SC 1461.

16 Arvind Datar, *Commentary on the Constitution of India* (New Delhi: LexisNexis Butterworths Wadhwa Nagpur, 2007), p. 1164.

17 Ibid.

High Court to the Andhra Pradesh High Court—challenged the constitutional validity of the presidential notification in a writ petition before the Gujarat High Court. The Gujarat High Court allowed the writ petition on the ground that the President had not effectively consulted the CJI in making the transfer. In 1976, the Union of India filed an appeal; the Supreme Court disposed it on the government's assurance that it would transfer Justice Sheth back to the Gujarat High Court.[18] However, though the outcome of this litigation was favourable to Justice Sheth, the Supreme Court refused to acknowledge that the consent of a high court judge was a necessary condition for his transfer to another high court, as a matter of principle. As a result, though the case vindicated Justice Sheth's stand, it did not question the legality of using transfers to punish independent judges.

Another unhappy practice developed—although vacancies were available for permanent judges, every high court judge was initially appointed as an additional judge before being confirmed as permanent. If the executive was unhappy with the decisions of a particular judge, he/she could be penalized by being refused confirmation as a permanent judge of that high court. This system clearly went against the principles of the Constitution, under which additional judges were to be appointed not as a matter of course, but only to meet temporary increase in business or work arrears.[19]

Before and during the Emergency, the government misused its powers to compromise the decisional independence of the courts. The powers of appointing and transferring judges were used to

---

18   *Union of India v. Sankalchand Himatlal Sheth* (AIR 1977 SC 2328).
19   *See* Article 224 of the Constitution.

punish and coerce independent judges who were unwilling to toe the government's line on policy matters. A different dimension to judicial independence—rather the lack of it—became a reality. This move to undermine judicial independence altered the course of Indian constitutional development forever.

What Started It All: The Law Minister's Circular

On 18 March 1981, P. Shivshankar, law minister of the Congress government (which had returned to power after a short stint by the Janata Party) issued a circular to the governor of Punjab and all state chief ministers (except those of the north-eastern states). This circular requested them to: (1) Obtain the consent of additional judges of the relevant state high court to be appointed as permanent judges in any other high court in India, and (2) Obtain the consent of people who would be offered judgeship in the future to be appointed initially in a court other than their state high court (*see* Appendix on page 184). While the circular was supposedly issued to 'further national integration' and 'combat narrow parochial tendencies', it was actually an attempt to further emasculate judicial independence, by subjecting the higher judiciary to greater political control.[20]

The country reacted. Public interest litigations (PILs) were filed. The constitutional validity of the law minister's circular was challenged. Writ petitions were also filed, some questioning the practice of appointing additional judges despite vacancies for permanent judges, others challenging the constitutionality of transferring certain judges from one high court to another.

---

20 Nani Palkhivala, *We, The People*, 23rd reprint (New Delhi: UBSPD, 2007), p. 226.

The Supreme Court clubbed[21] eight such writ petitions (broadly falling within three categories) filed in courts across India to hear the matter and dispose of each of these petitions in the seminal case of *S.P. Gupta v. President of India* (*First Judges Case*)[22] in December 1981. The case takes its title from the writ petition filed by advocate S.P. Gupta of the Allahabad High Court, concerning the appointment of three additional judges of that court.

Two Archaic Doctrines Eschewed: The Executive Has the Last Laugh

Each of the seven bench members issued a separate opinion in the *First Judges Case*, resulting in judgements that totalled nearly half a million words[23] and obscured, to some extent, the law on judicial appointments and transfers.[24] The government argued that since the writ petitions had been filed by senior advocates rather than the aggrieved parties (high court judges), the advocates had no locus standi[25] to move court. Until the late 1970s, the Supreme Court and high courts would entertain writ petitions only by people who were victims of an illegality or whose legal rights had been violated. However, in the *First*

---

21 Under Article 139A of the Constitution, where cases involving substantially the same questions of law are pending before two or more high courts or before the Supreme Court and high courts, the Supreme Court is empowered to dispose of all of the cases itself if it believes that they involve substantial questions of general importance.

22 AIR 1982 SC 149.

23 Palkhivala, *We, The People*, p. 222.

24 Granville Austin, *Working a Democratic Constitution: The Indian Experience* (New Delhi: Oxford University Press, 1999), p. 527.

25 'Locus standi' refers to the right to bring an action in a court and be heard by the court.

Judges Case, the PIL took firm root. Locus standi was extended—forever!

The Supreme Court refused to adhere to its strict rules of 'standing', holding that the 'cause of justice can never be allowed to be thwarted by any procedural technicalities'.[26] Each of the seven judges agreed on the right of the petitioners to bring the writ petitions. The Court laid down two liberal and salutary approaches to allow citizens to move the Supreme Court or high courts: (1) 'Representative standing', where a public-spirited citizen can file a writ petition to protect the poor, the downtrodden, and the economically or socially disadvantaged who are unable to effectively protect their rights, and (2) 'Citizen standing', where citizens can move court for the enforcement of public duties.[27] These principles formed the bedrock of public interest litigation in India and transformed the higher judiciary into an extremely important player in socioeconomic reforms and an integral part of decision-making—in an extended sense.

During the hearing, the petitioners requested the government to produce certain correspondence between the Union law minister, the CJI, and the Chief Justice of the Delhi High Court, which would have been vital to the court's conclusions. The government argued that such correspondence was protected by 'state privilege',[28] so the court could not ask for it. Rejecting this argument, the Supreme Court stated that transparency and openness are essential elements of a democratic society.

---

26 *First Judges Case* at para. 17 (judgement of Justice Bhagwati).

27 Michael G. Faure and A.V. Raja, 'Effectiveness of Environmental Public Interest Litigation in India: Determining the Key Variables', *Fordham Environmental Law Review*, vol. 21 (2010): p. 239.

28 A rule of evidence based on which unpublished official records of the state are protected from disclosure, as their disclosure may be injurious to public interest.

It ordered that the correspondence be produced, asserting that the 'right to know' how a nation is governed is an essential pillar of democracy. This affirmation by the Supreme Court was arguably one of the starting points of the right to information movement in India. Therefore, in the course of its judgement in the *First Judges Case*, the Supreme Court moved away from two traditional rules of law—the rule of locus standi and the protection of privileged communication—and laid down seminal roadmaps.

Moving to the crux of the court's decision, the majority held that judges could not be transferred from one high court to another as punishment. At the same time, the Supreme Court reiterated what it had said in Justice Sheth's case—the consent of a high court judge was not a necessary precondition for his transfer. The court also held that although an additional judge should usually be made permanent after the expiry of his interim term, confirmation as a permanent judge was not a right in itself.

The most important issue on which the court ruled in the *First Judges Case* was the dynamics of power between the executive and the judiciary in appointing judges. The court held that the CJI's opinion in appointing judges of the high court and Supreme Court was *not* to receive primacy. The CJI did not possess a veto in making judicial appointments. In fact, the majority gave the executive the final say in making appointments to the higher judiciary.[29] Interestingly, the majority also refused to strike down the law minister's circular, stating that it had 'no constitutional or legal sanction'.[30]

---

29 Singh, 'Securing the Independence of the Judiciary', p. 245.
30 *First Judges Case* at para. 44 (judgement of Justice Bhagwati).

First Judges Case: Good Journey, Bad Destination

The Supreme Court's decision in the *First Judges Case* was one of its many 'everybody wins' judgements of the 1970s and 1980s; it recognized an important doctrine (in favour of one party), but ultimately decided in favour of the opposing party.[31] It acknowledged that members of the bar had the right to file writ petitions in public interest, but yet it went ahead to make the government the final arbiter on appointments to the higher judiciary, thus upsetting the earlier balance of power between the judiciary and the government.

Ironically, the most significant contribution of the *First Judges Case* was not in the realm of judicial appointments. By broadening the narrow rule of locus standi, the court opened the floodgates to social action litigation, and India has never been the same since. Such litigation has been used for an incredibly diverse range of issues including the protection of women from custodial violence,[32] protection of slum and pavement dwellers,[33] preservation of the environment,[34] provision of immediate medical aid to accident victims[35] and protection of women from sexual harassment at the workplace.[36] The *First Judges Case* redefined the role of constitutional courts in India:[37]

---

31 Upendra Baxi, *Courage, Craft and Contention: The Indian Supreme Court in the Eighties* (Bombay: N.M. Tripathi, 1985), p. 38.

32 *Sheela Barse v. State of Maharashtra* (AIR 1983 SC 378).

33 *Olga Tellis v Bombay Municipal Corporation* (AIR 1986 SC 180).

34 *See*, for example, *Rural Litigation and Environment Kendra, Dehra Dun and Others v. State of U.P.* (AIR 1985 SC 652).

35 *Parmanand Katara v. Union of India* (AIR 1989 SC 2039).

36 *Vishaka v. State of Rajasthan* (AIR 1997 SC 3011).

37 Manoj Mate, 'Two Paths to Judicial Power: The Basic Structure Doctrine and Public Interest Litigation in Comparative Perspective', *San Diego International Law Journal*, vol. 12 (2010): p. 175.

the Supreme Court was transformed into the last bastion of hope for the poor[38] and is still seen the same way.

The court's ultimate verdict, however, ran contrary to constitutional convention.[39] It relegated the CJI to the position of an advisor and gave the substantial control over the judicial appointments process to the executive. Sadly, but knowingly, the Supreme Court compromised on its own independence. Although it 'developed the law in the right direction'[40] in many respects, the verdict was undesirable for India's democratic polity. From a position where the appointment power was balanced between the executive and the judiciary, the *First Judges Case* placed the executive in the driver's seat. Given that this occurred so soon after the Emergency, where the very same power of judicial appointments had been misused by the government to severely undermine judicial independence, one wonders why the court chose to compromise its independence by not retaining convention.

Second Judges Case: Drifting between Extremes

Public opinion was far from benign. The form of judicial appointments conceptualized in the *First Judges Case* continued for almost a decade, but meanwhile, public opinion was being mobilized against the decision. Academics called for an impartial system of judicial appointments, to be administered

---

38 Tayyab Mahmud, '"Surplus Humanity" and the Margins of Legality: Slums, Slumdogs, and Accumulation by Dispossession', *Chapman Law Review*, vol. 14 (2010): p. 1.

39 Nariman, *Before Memory Fades*, p. 390.

40 H.M. Seervai, *Constitutional Law of India*, 3rd ed. (Bombay: N.M. Tripathi, 1984), p. 2179.

by a collegial body consisting of members of the judiciary and the executive.[41] In the late 1980s, practising advocate Subhash Sharma, the Supreme Court Advocates-on-Record Association and the Honorary Secretary of the Bombay Bar Association[42] filed petitions before the Supreme Court asking for the vacancies of the judges of the Supreme Court and various high courts to be filled. While hearing the petitions, the Supreme Court observed that its decision in the *First Judges Case* merited reconsideration by a larger bench of judges.[43]

The questions on judicial appointments and transfers were therefore referred to a nine-judge bench of the Supreme Court in *Supreme Court Advocates-on-Record Association v. Union of India*[44] (*Second Judges Case*). Five separate opinions[45] were delivered by the bench and the majority overruled the earlier decision[46] of the Supreme Court in the *First Judges Case*.

The court emphasized that, under the Constitution, judicial appointments should be 'integrated, participatory and

---

41 Singh, 'Securing the Independence of the Judiciary', p. 245.

42 Established in 1862, an association of lawyers practising on the 'original side' of the Bombay High Court.

43 *Subhash Sharma v. Union of India* (AIR 1991 SC 631).

44 AIR 1994 SC 268.

45 The nine judges on the bench in the *Second Judges Case* were Justices S. Ratnavel Pandian, A.M. Ahmadi, Kuldip Singh, J.S. Verma, M.M. Punchhi, Yogeshwar Dayal, G.N. Ray, Dr A.S. Anand and S.P. Bharucha. Justice Verma spoke for himself and four other judges—this constituted the view of the majority on the bench. Justice Pandian and Justice Kuldip Singh wrote individual judgements agreeing with the majority view. Justice Punchhi took the view that in making judicial appointments, the CJI had primacy and that he was entitled to consult (or not to consult) any number of judges on the proposal. Justice Ahmadi dissented with the majority view, broadly adopting the reasoning used in the *First Judges Case*.

46 While the decision in the *First Judges Case* was pronounced by a bench of seven Supreme Court judges, the decision in the *Second Judges Case* was pronounced by a bench of nine Supreme Court judges.

consultative'. In an ideal scenario, there should be no scope for 'primacy' of the judiciary or the executive—both branches should make the appointments collectively, as originally contemplated by the Constitution. What the judgement effectively did was transfer the power of 'primacy' from the executive to the judiciary. So, when the government (via the President) and the CJI or chief justice of a high court conflicted over a particular judicial appointment, the Supreme Court in the *Second Judges Case* held that the latter's opinion would prevail.

And yet, while it secured primacy for the judiciary, the Supreme Court also sought to moderate its powers through the collegiate system. For appointments to the Supreme Court and high courts, the CJI was to decide after ascertaining the opinion of at least two of the most senior judges of the Supreme Court ('collegium' in the Supreme Court). For appointments of high court judges (where the chief justice of the relevant high court is also consulted), the chief justice of the high court was to decide after ascertaining the views of at least two of the most-senior judges of that high court (the 'collegium' in the relevant high court).

The *Second Judges Case* achieved the following in the area of judicial appointments: first, it overturned the decision in the *First Judges Case* and gave the last word on appointments to the judiciary; and second, it decentralized the power conferred upon the CJI/chief justice of the relevant high court by granting this power to a plurality of judges—the collegium.

On the issue of transfers of judges from one high court to another, the court held that the CJI's opinion would be decisive. However, on this issue as well, the court ensured decentralization of power by ruling that the CJI was to necessarily consult other judges whose opinion may be relevant before deciding to transfer a high court judge. Interestingly, though the court stuck to its position in the *First Judges Case* in finding that the consent of a high court judge was not a precondition for his transfer, it preserved its right to dictate!

Criticism of the Verdict in the *Second Judges Case*: Sacred Ritual with New Priests

The rationale behind the Supreme Court's judgement in the *Second Judges Case* was to minimize political influence in judicial appointments and reduce the individual discretion of the chief justices of the Supreme Court and high courts by introducing the decentralized, collegium system.[47] In effect, the Supreme Court moved from one extreme (the government making judicial appointments) to the other (judges becoming the supreme authority in the judicial appointments process). Why? Perhaps it was an overcompensation—an exaggerated remedial measure to rectify the 'self-inflicted wound'[48] caused by the Supreme Court's judgement in the *First Judges Case*.

There is no doubt that the decision in the *Second Judges Case* virtually rewrote some provisions of the Constitution.[49] The expression 'consultation' (with the CJI, in relation to appointing judges) was tactfully changed to 'concurrence'. What since? There

---

47 C.S. Vaidyanathan, 'Appointment of Judges to the Higher Judiciary' in *Constitutionalism Human Rights and the Rule of Law: Essays in Honour of Soli J Sorabjee,* eds Mool Chand Sharma and Raju Ramachandran (New Delhi: Universal Law Publishing, 2005), p. 193.

48 Datar, *Commentary on the Constitution of India*, p. 1153.

49 Durga Das Basu, *Shorter Constitution of India*, 13th ed. (Nagpur: Wadhwa Nagpur, 2001), p. 777.

is criticism of the high degree of opacity in the functioning of the collegium system. It has been criticized by insiders (judges who have been members of the collegium) as well as outsiders.[50] Senior advocate Fali S. Nariman, lead counsel for the petitioner (Supreme Court Advocates-on-Record Association) in the *Second Judges Case*, candidly said that this was a case he won, but one that he would 'prefer to have lost'.[51] In an interview, Justice J.S. Verma, author of the majority opinion in the *Second Judges Case*, lamented the manner in which the judgement was being implemented:

> My 1993 judgement . . . was very much misunderstood and misused . . . Therefore, some kind of rethink is required. My judgement says the appointment process of high court and Supreme Court judges is basically a joint or participatory exercise between the executive and the judiciary, both taking part in it.[52]

The judgement catalysed a shift in the balance of power, in favour of the judiciary. In the *First Judges Case,* Justice P.N. Bhagwati had this to say about the appointment power in question:

> Today the process of judicial appointments and transfers is shrouded in mystery. The public does not know how judges are selected and appointed or transferred and whether any, and if

50 Vaidyanathan, 'Appointment of Judges to the Higher Judiciary', p. 196.

51 Nariman, *Before Memory Fades*, p. 387.

52 Words of Justice J.S. Verma in V. Venkatesan, 'Interview with Justice J.S. Verma, former Chief Justice of India', *Frontline*, vol. 25, issue 20, 27 September 2008 -10 October 2008, http://www.frontline.in/navigation/?type=static&page=flonnet&rd url=fl2520/stories/20081010252003500.htm (accessed 28 November 2012).

so, what principles and norms govern this process. The exercise of the power of appointment and transfer remains a sacred ritual whose mystery is confined only to a handful of high priests . . . The mystique of this process is kept secret and confidential between just a few individuals, not more than two or four as the case may be, and the possibility cannot therefore be ruled out that howsoever highly placed may be these individuals, the process may on occasions result in the making of wrong appointments and transfers and may also at times, though fortunately very rare, lend itself to nepotism, political as well as personal and even trade-off.[53]

Unfortunately, later generations of Supreme Court judges have failed to heed Justice Bhagwati's lament. Despite judicial intervention in the *Second Judges Case*, the judicial appointment process remains as clandestine as it was in 1981. It remains, in every way, a mysterious sacred ritual—only the identity of the high priests has been altered.

Third Judges Case: Presidential Reference

The next confrontation between the judiciary and the executive over the issue of judicial appointments took place in 1997–98. The CJI, Justice M.M. Punchhi, recommended the names of five people for appointment to the Supreme Court. The executive refused to do so, expressing doubts about whether the recommended people were fit to be appointed as Supreme Court judges. As a result, President K.R. Narayanan sought the

---

53 *First Judges Case* at para. 84.

Supreme Court's opinion under Article 143[54] on nine questions, covering three broad issues: (1) Consultation between the CJI and his brother judges for deciding on appointments to the high courts and the Supreme Court, (2) Judicial review of the transfer of judges, and (3) The relevance of seniority of high court judges in making appointments to the Supreme Court.

A nine-judge bench of the Supreme Court delivered a unanimous opinion while answering the questions.[55] The court emphasized that judicial appointments would have to take place according to the principles enunciated in its decision in the *Second Judges Case*; the only revision it made was that for the appointment of judges to the Supreme Court, the collegium would consist of the CJI and four (as against two) senior-most colleagues. The judgement did not do much more than reiterate, endorse and perpetuate the collegium system of judicial appointments.

Lord Cooke of Thorndon, contributor to *Supreme But Not Infallible: Essays Written in Honour of the Supreme Court of India*,[56] used two quotes to summarize his views on the *Second Judges Case* and the *Third Judges Case*. To emphasize how divergent the *Second Judges Case* was from the actual constitutional text and intent, he quoted Shakespeare:

> *But man, proud man,*
> *Dressed in a little brief authority . . .*

---

54 Under Article 143 of the Constitution, the President is empowered to seek the opinion of the Supreme Court on important questions of law or fact that have arisen or are likely to arise.

55 *In Re: Under Article 143(1) of the Constitution of India* (AIR 1999 SC 1).

56 Lord Cooke of Thorndon, 'Where Angels Fear to Tread' in *Supreme But Not Infallible: Essays in Honour of the Supreme Court of India,* eds B.N. Kirpal et al. (New Delhi: Oxford University Press, 2000), p. 97.

Plays such fantastic tricks before high heaven
As make the angels weep

—William Shakespeare's *Measure for Measure*, Act II, Scene 2

To emphasize how debatable the decision in the *Third Judges Case* was, he quoted from Alexander Pope's poem titled *An Essay on Criticism*: 'For fools rush in, where angels fear to tread.'

Lord Cooke's observations aptly sum up the Supreme Court's actions in the *Second Judges Case* and the *Third Judges Case*. Through a fantastic constitutional interpretation, the Supreme Court rushed into uncharted constitutional territory, arrogating to itself the unprecedented power of carrying out judicial appointments. The decisions, though well-intentioned, have upset the balance of power as envisaged by our Constitution.

Who Will Watch the Watchers?

India has one of the most detailed constitutions in the world. It includes a chunk of administrative details to ensure that the constitutional process cannot be subverted. In spite of this, the judiciary has had to step in on many occasions to add to these details to ensure that the play in the joints provided by the makers of the Constitution was not misused. The appointments process is a paradigm example. In the spirit of the Constitution, the scheme of judicial appointments was meant to establish a system of checks and balances, where merit was the foremost consideration. If the executive had discussed, freely and frankly, with the CJI in all cases, without political compulsions or misaligned agendas, perhaps we would not have been struggling to find some sense of balance in the appointments procedure today.[57]

Within two decades, we have moved from one extreme to the other: from a judiciary controlled by the will of the executive to a judiciary with theoretically unbridled and unchecked power. Today, there is no institutionalized system of making recommendations for the appointment of judges.[58] The lack of transparency in the process has impacted the Supreme Court's legitimacy—a legitimacy it must desperately preserve, given the super-administrative role it has undertaken in the Indian democratic set-up.[59] Many who were closely associated with the *Second Judges Case* later expressed deep anguish at the effect of the judgement. Some say there is a real threat to the Indian judiciary from within.[60] Though most people would choose judge-controlled appointments as against politically controlled ones, it is time to attain a balance of power in selecting members of arguably the most powerful institution in India.

In constitutional theory, it is unprecedented to vest judicial appointment power in the Supreme Court.[61] In his book *The Least Dangerous Branch*, noted American jurist and law professor Alexander Bickel coined a term that now defines the nature of the judicial office. Bickel argued that the judicial role, by its very nature, was 'counter-majoritarian' and anti-democratic. He questioned the power of unelected, nominated judges to strike down laws passed by elected representatives of the people.

---

57 Arvind Datar, *Commentary on the Constitution of India*, p. 1160.

58 Nariman, *Before Memory Fades*, p. 398.

59 S.P. Sathe, 'Judicial Activism: The Indian Experience', *Washington University Journal of Law and Policy*, vol. 6 (2001): p. 29.

60 Shourie, *Mrs. Gandhi's Second Reign*, p. 249.

61 Lord Cooke of Thorndon, 'Where Angels Fear to Tread', p. 97.

While elected representatives are answerable to the people in periodic elections, judicial officers are nominated (not elected) and, once nominated, continue to rise through the hierarchy without being directly accountable to the people in any way. Yet, constitutions around the world empower an unelected judicial branch to review and invalidate actions of the elected branches of government.

Numerous constitutional law jurists have tried to resolve and answer the 'counter-majoritarian difficulty', but, over time, the judiciary's counter-majoritarian nature has been accepted as an unavoidable feature, which may be minimized if not completely resolved. In India's context, the Supreme Court exercises extensive powers in reviewing government actions and striking down (when necessary) laws and even constitutional amendments made by the Parliament. Yet, while judges in most other countries are appointed by independent commissions or by popularly elected governments, the Supreme Court's self-appointment power, coupled with its extensive powers, makes its counter-majoritarian character particularly pronounced.

As a way out, legal scholars have suggested creating a National Judicial Commission (composed of public functionaries from the judiciary and the executive), which would have the power to appoint judges of the higher judiciary.[62] The United Kingdom has introduced a similar process of judicial appointments following the Constitution Reform Act, 2005, whereby judicial appointments are made by an independent Judicial Appointments Commission comprising political, judicial and professional members. Similarly, the Consultative Council of

---

62 Janak Raj Jai, *Commissions and Omissions in the Administration of Justice* (New Delhi: Regency, 2003), p. 79.

European Judges in opinion titled 'Independence of the Judiciary and the Irremovability of Judges'[63] recommended that judicial appointments should be made by an independent authority on the basis of predetermined and publicized objective criteria to ensure transparency in the appointment process.

Proposals for a National Judicial Commission have been introduced in the Parliament on three separate occasions, but none has materialized. At this juncture, a commission of this nature seems to be the only solution to restore the system of checks and balances in judicial appointments and infuse transparency and accountability into the process.

---

63 Consultative Council of European Judges, Opinion No. 1 (2001), 23 November 2001, www.venice.coe.int/site/main/texts/JD_docs/CCJE_Opinion_1_E.htm (accessed on 31 October 2012).

APPENDIX

Circular issued by the Union law minister to the governor of Punjab and the chief ministers of all states (except the north-eastern states)[64]

D.O. No. 66/10/81-Jus.
Ministry of Law, Justice and Company Affairs, India
New Delhi – 110 001
March 18, 1981

My dear _____,

It has repeatedly been suggested to Government over the years by several bodies and forums including the States Reorganisation Commission, the Law Commission and various Bar Associations that to further national integration and to combat narrow parochial tendencies bred by caste, kinship and other local links and affiliations, one-third of the Judges of the High Court should as far as possible be from outside the State in which that High Court is situated. Somehow, no start could be made in the past in this direction. The feeling is strong, growing and justified that some effective steps should be taken very early in this direction.

2. In this context, I would request you to:

a) Obtain from all the Additional Judges working in the High Court of your State their consent to be appointed as permanent Judges in any other High Court in the country. They could, in addition, be requested to name three High Courts, in order

---

64 Reproduced from the judgement of the Supreme Court in the *First Judges Case.*

of preference, to which they would prefer to be appointed as permanent Judges; and

b) Obtain from persons who have already been or may in the future be proposed by you for initial appointment their consent to be appointed to any other High Court in the country along with a similar preference for three High Courts.

3. While obtaining the consent and the preference of the persons mentioned in paragraph 2 above, it may be made clear to them that the furnishing of the consent or the indication of a preference does not imply any commitment on the part at the Government either in regard to their appointment or in regard to accommodation in accordance with the preferences given.

4. I would be grateful if action is initiated very early by you and the written consent and preferences of all Additional Judges as well as of persons recommended by you for initial appointment are sent to me within a fortnight of the receipt of this letter.

5. I am also sending a copy of this letter to the Chief Justice of your High Court.

With regards,
Yours sincerely,
(P. Shivshankar)
Sd/-

To
1. Governor of Punjab
2. Chief Ministers (by name) (except north-eastern states)

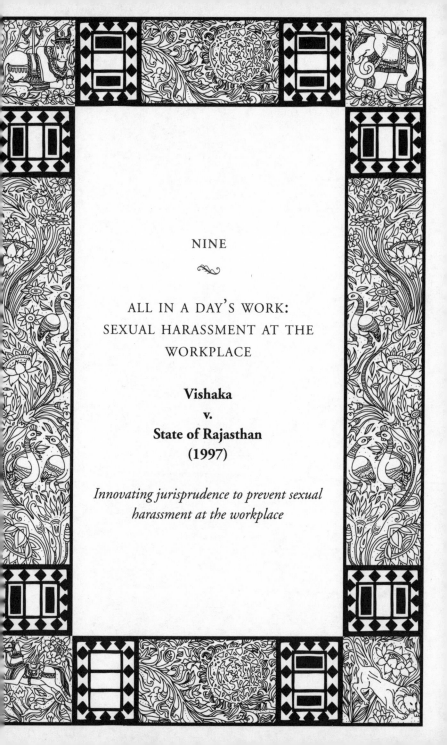

NINE

ALL IN A DAY'S WORK:
SEXUAL HARASSMENT AT THE
WORKPLACE

Vishaka
v.
State of Rajasthan
(1997)

Innovating jurisprudence to prevent sexual
harassment at the workplace

IN AN EMERGING Indian economy, as more and more women have started to work, the malady of sexual harassment at the workplace has reared its ugly head in several fields. From the police and the army to business process outsourcing set-ups, from multinational corporations to professional sport—it's regrettable that no sector or discipline has been spared. As has been the case with many other pressing issues, it was a Supreme Court decision that first brought this issue under sustained public scrutiny. Since the judgement, there have been several attempts (one pending, others failed) to make definitive laws on the subject.

In the context of sexual harassment, judicial activism reached its pinnacle in *Vishaka v. State of Rajasthan*[1] (*Vishaka*). The judgement was unprecedented for several reasons: the Supreme Court acknowledged and relied to a great extent on international treaties that had not been transformed into municipal law; the Supreme Court provided the first authoritative definition of 'sexual harassment' in India; and confronted with a statutory vacuum, it went creative and proposed the route of 'judicial legislation'.

---

1   AIR 1997 SC 3011.

Gang Rape of Bhanwari Devi

The trigger that led to a public interest litigation (PIL) being filed in respect of the *Vishaka* case was the gang rape of a social worker in Rajasthan. Bhanwari Devi was a *saathin*, a grass-roots worker and activist, employed in the Women's Development Project (WDP) of the government of Rajasthan. In 1992, the Rajasthan government launched a campaign against child marriage, in connection with which WDP employees persuaded villagers to abandon the practice, which was and still is rampant in Rajasthan. Bhanwari Devi made a spirited effort to prevent the marriage of a one-year-old girl, but in vain. What ensued was a complete breakdown of the institutional machinery in Rajasthan. The villagers harassed, threatened and socially boycotted Bhanwari Devi.[2] Then, in September 1992, five villagers raped her in the presence of her husband. She sought justice, but faced innumerable hurdles from police authorities. The trial court in Rajasthan went ahead and acquitted the five accused.

This spurred a group of five NGOs, under the name 'Vishaka', to file a PIL in the Supreme Court seeking detailed directions on how sexual harassment of women at the workplace could be prevented through a judicial process.

Thinking Global, Acting Local: Reference to International Treaties

The Constitution of India does not have a precise stand on the value of international treaties that have been signed or ratified

---

2   Avani Mehta Sood, 'Part II Equality, Social Exclusion, and Women's Rights: Redressing Women's Rights Violations Through the Judiciary', *Jindal Global L Review*, vol. 1 (2009): p. 137.

by the government, but not implemented via legislation.[3] In *Vishaka*, the court moved towards a more purposive understanding of fundamental rights by affirming that '[a]ny International Convention not inconsistent with the fundamental rights and in harmony with its spirit must be read into these provisions [the fundamental rights] to enlarge the meaning and content thereof, to promote the object of the constitutional guarantee'.[4] Since there was no legislation in India related to sexual harassment at the workplace, the court stated that it was free to rely on the Convention on the Elimination of All Forms of Discrimination against Women (CEDAW—signed by India in 1980) in interpreting Articles 14, 15, 19 and 21[5] of the Constitution. To justify its decision the court referred to several sources including the Beijing Statement of Principles of the Independence of the Judiciary,[6] a decision of the High Court of Australia[7] and its own earlier decisions.[8]

---

3   Article 51(c) of the Constitution reads: 'The State shall endeavour to foster respect for international law and treaty obligations in the dealing of organized peoples with one another.'

4   *Vishaka* at para. 7.

5   Broadly, these fundamental rights comprise the following: Article 14 of the Constitution: right to equality before the law; Article 15 of the Constitution: prohibition of discrimination on grounds of religion, race, caste, sex or place of birth; Article 19 of the Constitution: the six freedoms (previously seven) including freedom of speech and expression and freedom to assemble peaceably without arms; and Article 21 of the Constitution: protection of life and personal liberty.

6   The Supreme Court asserted that its obligation to enforce fundamental rights must be viewed in the context of the Beijing Statement of Principles of the Independence of the Judiciary, which emphasizes the judiciary's role to protect and observe human rights and promote the rule of law.

7   *Minister for Immigration and Ethnic Affairs v. Tech* ((1995) 128 ALR 353); in this case, the court alluded to the people's 'legitimate expectation' that it will observe international law in case there is no contrary domestic legislation.

8   *Nilabati Behera v. State of Orissa* (AIR 1993 SC 1960).

Vishaka also reflected a productive interaction between international covenants and municipal courts.[9] Since *Vishaka*, the Supreme Court has (had to) increasingly rely upon multilateral treaties, particularly those forming a part of the International Bill of Rights,[10] because of the long periods of legislative inactivity in spheres of contemporary relevance. Given that all decisions of the Supreme Court are treated as law under Article 141[11] of the Constitution, the guidelines issued by the court in *Vishaka* plugged a legislative vacuum.

Guidelines or Legislation?

The Supreme Court then issued a series of 'guidelines' (based on CEDAW) to protect women from sexual harassment at the workplace. These guidelines were to be 'strictly observed in all workplaces' (whether in the private or public sector) and would be 'binding and enforceable in law' until suitable laws were made on the issue.[12]

The Supreme Court set out the following significant guidelines:

1.   The employer and/or other responsible people in a workplace are duty-bound to prevent or deter sexual harassment and set up processes to resolve, settle, or prosecute in such cases.

---

9   Martha C. Nussbaum, 'India: Implementing Sex Equality Through Law', *Chicago Journal of International Law*, vol. 2 (2001): p. 35.

10   The International Bill of Rights is an informal name for the Universal Declaration of Human Rights (1948), the International Covenant on Civil and Political Rights (1966) and the International Covenant on Economic, Social and Cultural Rights (1966).

11   Article 141 of the Constitution reads: 'The law declared by the Supreme Court shall be binding on all courts within the territory of India.'

12   *Vishaka* at para. 12.

2. For the first time in India, 'sexual harassment' was defined authoritatively. The Supreme Court stated that it includes 'such unwelcome sexually determined behaviour (whether directly or by implication) such as: physical contact and advances, a demand or request for sexual favours, sexually coloured remarks, showing pornography, and any other unwelcome physical, verbal or non-verbal conduct of sexual nature'.[13]

3. All employers or persons in charge of workplaces must strive to prevent sexual harassment and, if any act amounts to a specific offence under the Indian Penal Code, 1860[14] (the IPC) or any other law, they must take appropriate action to punish the guilty.

4. Even if the act is not considered a legal offence or a breach of service rules, the employer should create appropriate mechanisms so that the complaint is addressed and redressed in a time-bound manner.

5. This complaint mechanism must, if necessary, provide a complaints committee, a special counsellor or other support service, such as assuring confidentiality. The complaints committee should be headed by a woman, and at least half its members must be women. Also, to pre-empt any undue pressure from senior levels, the complaints committee must involve a third party (such as an NGO) familiar with the challenges of sexual harassment.

---

13 *Vishaka* at para. 16.

14 For example, assaulting/using criminal force with the intent of outraging the modesty of a woman (Section 354 of the IPC) or rape (Sections 375, 376 of the IPC).

6. The employer must sensitize female employees to their rights and prominently notify the court's guidelines.
7. Even if a third party is responsible for sexual harassment, the employer must take all steps necessary to support the victim.
8. The central and state governments should adopt suitable measures to ensure that private sector employers implement the guidelines.

Some authors have correctly observed that *Vishaka* has 'institutionalized judicial lawmaking'.[15] Although they are susceptible to euphemism,[16] the court's guidelines are as good as laws and the court intended that they would be operated, at least in theory, in the same manner as statutes. This is reinforced by the fact that the Supreme Court's decisions are 'law' and are legally binding on all other Indian courts, under Article 141 of the Constitution.[17] The mere fact that the guidelines were transitory does not affect this deduction; after all, the legislation that Parliament enacts itself operates until Parliament decides that it should not.[18] Therefore, rather than temporarily filling a legislative void, what the Supreme Court really did was redress

---

15 *See*, for instance, Shubhankar Dam, 'Lawmaking Beyond Lawmakers: Understanding the Little Right and the Great Wrong (Analysing the Legitimacy of the Nature of Judicial Lawmaking in India's Constitutional Dynamic)', *Tulane Journal of International and Comparative Law*, vol. 13 (2005): p. 109.

16 *U.S. Verma, Principal and Delhi Public School Society v. National Commission for Women and Ors.* (163 (2009) DLT 557), where the Delhi High Court referred to the guidelines propounded in *Vishaka* as a 'sequel' to the Supreme Court's declaration that gender-based unacceptable behaviour was contrary to Articles 15 and 21 of the Constitution.

17 Article 141 of the Constitution reads: 'The law declared by the Supreme Court shall be binding on all courts within the territory of India.'

18 Moreover, the guidelines that the Supreme Court framed as makeshift guidelines have now been in force for thirteen years as the only 'law' on sexual harassment at the workplace!

a democratic deficit. One wonders whether this is what Cardozo envisioned when he posited that 'judges don't discover law, they create it'![19]

Horizontal Application of Fundamental Rights

Recently, it has been argued[20] that *Vishaka* represents the 'horizontal' application of fundamental rights.[21] Under the Constitution, fundamental rights are usually enforced only 'vertically'[22] against the state, except certain rights, such as the right against untouchability,[23] which also operate 'horizontally' against other citizens.[24] Having said that, it is also a fact that most fundamental rights are worded ambiguously—it is unclear whether they can be invoked in case non-state actors violate them. The *Vishaka* decision fits perfectly within what noted Harvard law professor and constitutional jurist Mark Tushnet

---

19 Benjamin Cardozo, *The Nature of the Judicial Process*, 1st printed ed. (Yale University Press, 1921).

20 *See* Tanurabh Khaitan, 'Make Them Pay for it', *The Telegraph*, 21 June 2005, www.telegraphindia.com/1050621/asp/opinion/story_4871199.asp (accessed 12 January 2013); also *see* International Commission of Jurists, 'Access to Justice: Human Rights Abuses Involving Corporations', p. 7, www.icj.org/dwn/database/AccesstoJustice-India-ElecDist-July2011.pdf (accessed 10 January 2013).

21 The 'horizontal' application of fundamental rights refers to a situation where a person may seek to enforce his/her fundamental rights in case of a violation of the same by a private body.

22 The 'vertical' approach considers the enforcement of fundamental rights in cases of violation by state action.

23 Article 17 of the Constitution of India reads: 'Abolition of Untouchability—Untouchability is abolished and its practice in any form is forbidden. The enforcement of any disability arising out of "Untouchability" shall be an offence punishable in accordance with law.'

24 *See* Sudhir Krishnaswamy, *Horizontal Application of Fundamental Rights and State Action in India in Human Rights, Justice and Empowerment*, 2nd ed. (New Delhi: Oxford University Press, 2009), p. 47.

calls 'residual State-action horizontality'—the 'horizontal' application of fundamental rights in cases where there is a legislative vacuum,[25] as was the case in *Vishaka*.

Developments after *Vishaka*

Dozens of cases have cropped up across high courts (and occasionally in the Supreme Court too) with reference to the *Vishaka* guidelines; these seek the establishment of complaints committees, dispute the constitution of complaints committees where they have already been in place, or challenge orders of dismissal based on the decisions of these committees.

Apparel Export Promotion Council v. A.K. Chopra[26] (*Chopra*) was the first case, in 1999, where the Supreme Court found an opportunity to follow its judgement in *Vishaka*. The council's chairman was accused of sexually harassing his secretary; though he made repeated attempts, the chairman never actually molested her. On her complaint, however, his services were terminated. When he filed a writ petition against 'his employer', the Delhi High Court found that since the chairman did not make any physical contact with his secretary, he did actually not molest her.[27] In appeal by the council, the Supreme Court reversed the Delhi High Court's judgement, recognizing that physical contact was not a prerequisite of sexual harassment, given its

---

25 *See* Mark Tushnet, *Weak Courts, Strong Rights*, 1st paperback ed. (Princeton: Princeton University Press, 2008), p. 207

26 AIR 1999 SC 625.

27 Louise Feld, 'Along the Spectrum of Women's Rights Advocacy: A Cross-Cultural Comparison of Sexual Harassment Law in the United States and India', *Fordham International Law Journal*, vol. 25 (2002), p. 1205.

broad definition in *Vishaka*. It asserted that sexual harassment compromised the dignity of women and cannot be condoned. In addition to the international sources referred to in *Vishaka*, the court also cited the International Covenant on Economic, Social and Cultural Rights and the International Labour Organization's seminar on combating sexual harassment at work.[28]

The Supreme Court's refreshingly progressive approach in *Chopra* marked a transition in the usual stance of Indian courts. The apex court acknowledged that harassment transcends physical barriers and that the effects of mental harassment can be equally damaging. And yet the courts' deep-seated insensitivity to women's issues still shows up occasionally; the most recent example was a case where the Supreme Court was severely criticized for referring to an unmarried partner as a 'keep' in a case under the Protection of Women from Domestic Violence Act, 2005.[29]

In *D.S. Grewal v. Vimmi Joshi*,[30] a colonel of the Indian Army made advances at and wrote inappropriate letters to the principal of an army public school. The principal was apprehensive that if she objected to his conduct, he would create a hostile working environment and hinder her employment, including her promotion. Her fears did come true as her services were terminated. The Supreme Court ordered the school management to constitute a three-member complaints committee (as mandated in the *Vishaka* guidelines) to ascertain if there were a

---

28 International Labour Organization Tripartite Regional Seminar on Combating Sexual Harassment at Work, Manila, November 1993.

29 *D. Velusamy v. D. Patchaiammal* (2010 (4) KLT 384 (SC)) (Supreme Court of India).

30 (2009) 2 SCC 210.

prima facie case against the army officer. If the committee found such a case, it would submit its report to the army, which would then initiate disciplinary proceedings.

The court also affirmed that the school management was bound to bear the legal costs incurred by the principal (with counsel fee assessed at 50,000 rupees), for it had not complied with the *Vishaka* guidelines to begin with. In the absence of laws on sexual harassment at the workplace, perhaps imposing additional real-time costs would catalyse employers into adhering to the *Vishaka* guidelines, apart from the loss of reputation that they may face if they fail to do so.

Courts have emphasized that all employers must strictly comply with the *Vishaka* guidelines and have not viewed alternative mechanisms (in lieu of complaints committees) very kindly. In a case where a public company appointed an advocate as an inquiry officer to investigate a complaint of sexual harassment, the Bombay High Court refused to accept the efficacy of the procedure and held that the complaints mechanism postulated in *Vishaka* was mandatory.[31]

Courts have been quite sensitive to issues arising from the *Vishaka* guidelines. Recognizing that the guidelines apply to all cooperative societies and private institutions, the Kerala High Court observed that 'the quality of womanhood does not change by the place where she works, be it public or private.'[32] In yet another shift of stance, the Madras High Court held that even in cases where the allegation of harassment appeared baseless

---

31 *Arati Durgaram Gavandi v. Managing Director, Tata Metaliks Limited* (2008 (6) Bom CR 1) (Bombay High Court); *see* also *Dr. Punita K. Sodhi* v. *Union of India & Ors.* ((2011) 1 LLJ 371 Del) (Delhi High Court).

32 *Puthuppan v. K.S. Girija* (2008 (3) KLJ 416) (Kerala High Court).

and seemed like an afterthought, the proper course would be to refer the matter to the complaints committee.[33]

On analysing Indian jurisprudence after *Vishaka*, it is clear that the Indian judicial system has treated sexual harassment with seriousness; it has defined harassment inclusively and covers any behaviour that denies a person employment-related benefits due to rejection of sexual demands (quid pro quo harassment) or creates a hostile work environment (without directly impacting on economic and other benefits).

A Double-Edged Weapon

Any measure that aims to protect disadvantaged sections of society or minorities is likely to be abused, and *Vishaka* is no exception. In the case of *Usha C.S. v. Madras Refineries*[34] (*Madras Refineries*), the Madras High Court heard a complaint of sexual harassment made by an employee of Madras Refineries Ltd, a public sector undertaking. The employee alleged that she was denied her study-leave with pay, salary and promotion because she rejected the advances of the general manager of her department. After examining the facts the court held that the employee's allegations regarding her promotion and study-leave were baseless, as both decisions appeared to have been taken in accordance with company policy. Further, a complaints committee had been properly constituted, but the employee had persistently delayed the inquiry; therefore, her allegation of sexual harassment was merely a weapon to bargain for a promotion and study-leave with pay, contrary to company policy. Highlighting

33 *K. Narmatha v. Home Secretary* ((2011) 1 MLJ 495) (Madras High Court).
34 (2001) 1 MLJ 802.

and condemning the misuse of the Supreme Court's judgement in *Vishaka*, the court held:

> The employer, who is supposed to keep a vigilant eye on the victim and the delinquent, is not expected to allow the women to use the shield so presented by the apex court as a weapon to wreak vengeance. It is true that we are bound by the directions of the apex court, but that does not mean that they can be allowed to be interpreted to suit the convenience of the woman like the petitioner, for personal gain.[35]

The court thereafter described *Vishaka* as a 'double-edged weapon'. In keeping with other decisions on the subject, it affirmed that the court cannot assume that an allegation of harassment is correct unless it is first referred to a complaints committee.

Though the court's ultimate view was sound, one of its observations is questionable:

> The petitioner/appellant before us is not an ordinary working woman; instead she was carrying on the Research by joining the Ph.D. course. Had there been any harassment, much less a sexual harassment, a woman like the petitioner would not have kept quiet for a period of about six years.[36]

The argument that a woman pursuing a research degree would face less pressure in making a complaint as opposed to an

---

35 *Madras Refineries* at para. 22.
36 Ibid., para. 24.

'ordinary working woman' is not at all convincing. Well-educated women are also hesitant to report harassment as they are equally prone to any vengeful act that the 'harasser' may resort to.

Can the Judiciary be an Interim Parliament?

Many argue that the Supreme Court encroached on the legislature's jurisdiction in *Vishaka*. What the court essentially did was frame a set of guidelines that would operate until laws were made, since neither the legislature nor the executive exercised its constitutional duty to do so. Interestingly, a two-judge bench of the Supreme Court was diametrically opposed on whether judges can play parliamentarians in *University of Kerala v. Council, Principals', Colleges, Kerala and Ors.*[37] (*University of Kerala*). Justice Markandey Katju opined that there were 'hundreds of pressing social needs', but it was not within the court's domain to address them just because there were no laws related to them. He also made some striking observations on the Supreme Court's role in *Vishaka*:

> In *Vishaka v. State of Rajasthan* . . . a three-judge bench of this court has issued various directives and as stated therein these will be treated as law under Article 141 of the Constitution . . . While we fully agree that working women should be protected against sexual harassment, the constitutional question remains whether such directives by this court are constitutionally valid? In substance the court has said . . . that it will become an interim Parliament and legislate on the subject until Parliament makes a law . . . Is this constitutionally valid? Can the court convert

---

37 AIR 2010 SC 2532.

itself into an interim Parliament and make law until Parliament makes a law on the subject? I have grave doubts about this.[38]

On the other hand, Justice Ashok Kumar Ganguly said that judicial intervention is permissible in situations where there is a legislative void, that accomplished jurists share this opinion,[39] and that the cases where the Supreme Court played such a proactive role were 'applauded internationally'.[40] He also cited examples of how the court had eschewed technicalities[41] (such as the strict rule of standing).

As the bench was divided on the validity of 'judicial legislation' and as it involved a substantial question of law, related to interpreting the Constitution itself, the matter was placed before the Chief Justice of India for reference to a Constitution Bench of the Supreme Court. The judgement of Justice Katju and Justice Ganguly referring the matter to a Constitution Bench was passed on 11 November 2009. The reference before the Chief Justice is still pending.

A question that is bound to arise is whether the Supreme Court is competent to frame binding guidelines as it did in *Vishaka*. If the Supreme Court answers in the negative, India may once again find itself without a law relating to sexual harassment at the workplace, considering that a number of bills on the subject have been drafted in the last decade, but to no avail.

---

38   *University of Kerala*, p. 10.

39   Richard A. Posner, *The Federal Courts: Crisis and Reform*, 1st ed. (Cambridge: Harvard University Press, 1985), p. 3.

40   N.W. Barber, 'Prelude to the Separation of Powers', *The Cambridge Law Journal*, vol. 60 (2001): p. 59.

41   *Vineet Narain v. Union of India* (AIR 1998 SC 889); *Vellore Citizens' Forum v. Union of India* (AIR 1996 SC 2715).

One aspect the Supreme Court overlooked when delivering its judgement in *University of Kerala* was that in its earlier decision in *Vishaka*, the court did not impose its own views but applied the doctrine of incorporation, under which international law becomes a part of municipal law if they are not at odds. This was not the case in the facts before the Supreme Court in *University of Kerala*. The Constitution Bench can demarcate between the legislative realm and the judicial realm based on the finding that when confronted with a legislative vacuum, the court can apply only the established rules of international law—not its own conception of what the law should be—until laws are framed by the legislature.

Legislative Inaction

Vishaka was intended to be an interim measure which would apply until the Parliament enacted laws to protect women from being sexually harassed at workplaces. Since the judgement, the National Commission for Women (NCW) has prepared a Code of Conduct for the Workplace[42] as well as draft bills on the subject in 2000, 2003, 2004, 2006[43] and 2010.

In December 2010, the Protection of Women against Sexual Harassment at Workplace Bill, 2010 was tabled in Parliament.[44]

---

42 *See* Vandana Shiva, *Sexual Violence against Women: Penal Law and Human Rights Perspectives* (New Delhi: LexisNexis Butterworths Wadhwa, 2009), p. 489.

43 The Sexual Harassment of Women at their Workplace (Prevention) Bill, 2000; the Sexual Harassment of Women at their Workplace (Prevention) Bill, 2003; the Sexual Harassment of Women at the Workplace (Prevention and Redressal) Bill, 2004; and the Sexual Harassment of Women at Workplace (Prevention, Prohibition and Redressal) Bill, 2006 (all) fell through at different stages.

44 'Bill to prevent workplace sexual harassment tabled', *The Hindu*, 7 December 2010, www.thehindu.com/news/national/article937482.ece (accessed 10 January 2013).

The bill features many progressive measures to redress sexual harassment: monetary penalty for employers, interim relief for complainants and compulsory reporting procedures for organizations. Interestingly, the bill does not necessitate an employer–employee relationship; so, it actually protects not only employees but also clients, customers, apprentices, daily wagers, students and hospital patients. Initially, the bill did not include the domestic workforce—among the most vulnerable segments of the unorganized sector in India—and was sharply criticized for failing to do so; it has now been amended to overcome this lacuna. Yet, even as the bill addresses the more pressing issue of sexual harassment against women at the workplace, it is still non-inclusive because it does not take into account such harassment against men. This category of harassment is rare, but not unheard of. On the whole, the bill is a step in the right direction—it has been passed by both houses of Parliament[45] and received Presidential assent on 25 April 2013.[46]

Why We Need Comprehensive Legislation

Vishaka was a seminal judgement because the Supreme Court's ruling ended the debate over whether sexual harassment of women at the workplace was a real problem. *Vishaka* is still the only pan-India law on this specific issue.

---

45 'Parliament passes sexual harassment at workplace bill', *Times of India*, 27 February 2013, http://articles.timesofindia.indiatimes.com/2013-02-27/india/37330220_1_physical-contact-and-advances-conduct-of-sexual-nature-sexually-coloured-remarks (accessed 1 March 2013).

46 *See* Press Information Bureau, Ministry of Law & Justice, Government of India, 'The Sexual Harassment of Women at Workplace (Prevention, Prohibition and Redressal) Act, 2013: Published in The Gazette of India', press release, 25 April 2013, http://pib.nic.in/newsite/erelease.aspx?relid=95069 (accessed 30 April 2013).

A writ petition currently pending in the Supreme Court seeks proper enforcement of the *Vishaka* guidelines by private and public institutions.[47] The Supreme Court has passed several orders in this petition—a significant one directing the labour commissioners of all states to take steps to implement the guidelines. Not much has changed at the grass roots though.[48]

A recent survey by the Centre for Transforming India suggests that nearly 88 per cent of the female workforce in information technology as well as business/knowledge process outsourcing companies have reported facing some form of workplace sexual harassment.[49] What is worrying is that 47 per cent of the employees did not know where to report this harassment, 91 per cent did not report for fear of being victimized and 77 per cent said that they were not sensitized to sexual harassment policies as part of their hiring process. Recent reports indicate that paramilitary forces do not adhere to guidelines on sexual harassment either.[50]

Unfortunately, despite the strides made by *Vishaka*, most employers are yet to constitute complaints committees. Experience

47 *Medha Kotwal Lele* v. *Union of India* (WP (Crl.) Nos 173-177/1999) (Supreme Court of India); taking taking a cue from this writ petition, the Maharashtra State Commission for Women wrote to all state authorities and public sector undertakings in Maharashtra requesting them to comply with the requirements laid down in *Vishaka*.

48 Subhradipta Sarkar, 'The Quest for Victims' Justice in India', *Human Rights Brief*, vol. 17 (2010): p. 16.

49 Aarti Dhar, '88% women subjected to sexual harassment at workplace in IT sector, reveals survey', *The Hindu*, 12 November 2010, www.thehindu.com/todays-paper/tp-national/88-women-subjected-to-sexual-harassment-at-workplace-in-it-sector-reveals-survey/article881444.ece (accessed 14 March 2013).

50 Aarti Dhar, 'Paramilitary forces not adhering to norms on sexual harassment, says House panel', *The Hindu*, 4 December 2010, www.thehindu.com/todays-paper/tp-national/paramilitary-forces-not-adhering-to-norms-on-sexual-harassment-says-house-panel/article930870.ece (accessed 13 March 2013).

shows that such committees are often constituted only when a court orders so in a particular case. Hence, the *Vishaka* guidelines have operated as a remedial rather than preventive measure. A recent statistic revealed that most women are not aware of the Supreme Court's judgement in *Vishaka*.[51] This underscores how important it is to make laws on the subject as that would provide machinery for the systematic prevention and redressal of sexual harassment of women at the workplace. While *Vishaka* is only enforced from case to case, a law would be enforced in all cases. Only when there is comprehensive legislation can the workplace be truly and completely gender-sensitized to meet the aspiration of a harassment-free work environment.

51 Sucheta Dalal, 'Bias in the Boardroom', *The Sunday Express*, 18 May 2003, www.indianexpress.com/storyOld.php?storyId=24079 (accessed 13 March 2013).

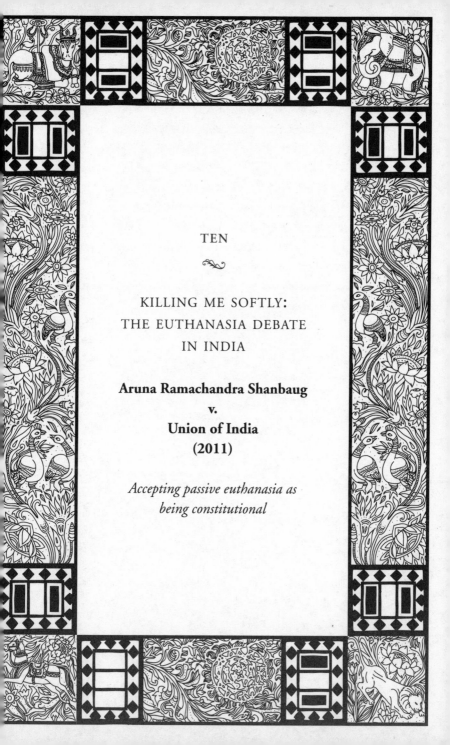

TEN

KILLING ME SOFTLY:
THE EUTHANASIA DEBATE
IN INDIA

Aruna Ramachandra Shanbaug
v.
Union of India
(2011)

Accepting passive euthanasia as
being constitutional

DOES A TERMINALLY ILL person have the right to hasten his death by asking for either his medical treatment to be withdrawn or for a lethal injection to be administered to end his suffering? Do the relatives of a patient, who has been in a permanently vegetative state for so long that she has almost no hope of recovery, have the right to ask for her life-support system to be switched off? This chapter highlights the journey of the judicial system into the highly sensitive and much debated issue of euthanasia.

Euthanasia is a complex ethical issue on which everyone has an opinion: from a child in Class 6 to a media baron of sixty. But the euthanasia issue gets even trickier when it comes to formulating law. Why? Because this is an area where questions of law grapple with moral and ethical values unlike any other. Until 2011, all forms of euthanasia were illegal in India, irrespective of manner, purpose and motive. Even so, euthanasia had and still has many 'silent supporters' in the medical profession.[1] So, when a journalist moved the Supreme Court of India in *Aruna Ramachandra Shanbaug v. Union of India*[2] (*Aruna Shanbaug*), asking it to allow a sixty-three-year-old nurse who had spent more than half her life in a vegetative state to die peacefully, the court stepped in to answer a question even though it felt like 'a ship in an uncharted sea'.

---

1   Lily Srivastava, *Law & Medicine* (New Delhi: Universal Law Publishing, 2010), p. 152.
2   (2011) 1 SCALE 673.

Suicide Law and the 'Right to Die'

What is the difference between euthanasia and suicide? This is tough to answer because the two concepts are very closely interlinked and the dividing line between them is very thin. Euthanasia denotes causing the death of incurable or terminally-ill patients; and the meaning of suicide is universally known. It is hard to imagine a legal system where the relatives of a patient in a vegetative state can decide to end his life while a fully competent adult is not allowed to end his own.

An attempt to commit suicide is a criminal offence in India, punishable with imprisonment of up to one year and a fine under Section 309 of the Indian Penal Code, 1860 (the IPC). It is a unique offence—if you fail, you are punished, but if you succeed, you are not—since, of course, a 'successful' suicide means that there is no one to punish. Those who abet suicide can be imprisoned for up to ten years and fined under Section 306 of the IPC. For a long time, this was the only safeguard against the instigation of *sati*[3] in India.

The law penalizing suicide attempts has been widely criticized over the last few decades. As early as 1971, the Law Commission of India recommended that Section 309 of the IPC, a 'harsh and unjustifiable' provision, should be deleted.[4] It has also been

---

3   An ancient Hindu custom according to which a widow was expected to immolate herself at the funeral pyre of her husband. Although it is now illegal, it is still prevalent in certain parts of India.

4   Law Commission of India, '42nd Report on Indian Penal Code', 1971, p. 244, http://lawcommissionofindia.nic.in/1-50/Report42.pdf (accessed 29 january 2013); also *see* Law Commission of India, '210th Report on Humanization and Decriminalization of Attempt to Suicide', 2008, http://lawcommissionofindia.nic.in/reports/report210.pdf (accessed 30 January 2013), which again suggested the repeal of Section 309 of the IPC.

constitutionally challenged several times before high courts and the Supreme Court. The Delhi High Court once observed that it was a '[s]trange paradox that in the age of votaries of euthanasia, suicide should be criminally punishable'.[5]

In 1985, *Maruti Dubal v. State of Maharashtra*[6] (*Maruti Dubal*), a police constable was so despondent with the inaction of government authorities that he tried to immolate himself outside the office of Bombay's municipal commissioner. When criminal charges were pressed against him, he challenged Section 309 of the IPC in the Bombay High Court, saying that it violates Articles 14[7] and 21[8] of the Constitution. The court accepted the challenge and agreed that there was 'nothing unnatural about the desire to die'.[9] It also said that every man is the master of his own body and has the right to deal with it as he pleases. A person who attempts suicide, whether due to mental disorder or physical ailment, needs treatment and care more than imprisonment. The court concluded that the constitutional right to live includes the 'right not to live' or the right to end one's life.[10] The Bombay High Court held that Section 309 was ultra vires or 'beyond the powers' of the Constitution and struck it down. All prosecutions instituted against the petitioner under Section 309 were quashed.

However, in a case in the following year, the Andhra Pradesh High Court upheld the constitutionality of Section 309 of

---

5 *State v. Sanjay Kumar Bhatia* ((1986) 10 DRJ 31 at para. 1) (Delhi High Court).
6 (1986) MhLJ 913 (Bombay High Court).
7 The right to equality.
8 The right to life and personal liberty.
9 *Maruti Dubal* at para. 11.
10 Ibid., para. 10.

the IPC.[11] The court found that a law punishing an attempt to commit suicide was an important tool in the age of hunger strikes and self-immolation threats. It also held that not every case under Section 309 would necessarily result in punishment or imprisonment; the section only defined the upper limits of possible punishment.

Is it constitutionally permissible to penalize suicide? This question arose in the Supreme Court in *P. Rathinam v. Union of India*[12] (*Rathinam*). Hearing the writ petition challenging the constitutional validity of Section 309, the court rightly held that an attempt to commit suicide indicated a psychological problem rather than any criminal instinct. After weighing every possible legal and moral implication of treating a suicide attempt as a criminal offence, the court struck down Section 309 of the IPC as being void and ineffectual. In fact, the court held that Section 309 contravened the right to life under Article 21.

The Supreme Court's judgement in *Rathinam* did not hold for long. In *Gian Kaur v. State of Punjab*[13] (*Gian Kaur*), a married couple appealed against their conviction for abetting suicide under Section 306. They argued that since the 'right to die' fell within the ambit of the right to life under Article 21 (as the Supreme Court held in *Rathinam*), a person who helped another commit suicide would merely be facilitating the enforcement of a fundamental right, implying that Section 306 of the IPC which penalized abetment of suicide, was also unconstitutional.

---

11 *Chenna Jagadeeswar v. State of Andhra Pradesh* (1988 Cr.L.J. 549) (Andhra Pradesh High Court)
12 AIR 1994 SC 1844.
13 AIR 1996 SC 1257.

This logic was clearly flawed and the Supreme Court rejected the argument, and rightly so. However, it also overruled its earlier judgement in *Rathinam*[14] and ruled afresh that the constitutional right to life did not include the right to die. So, Section 309 was once again held to be constitutionally valid and effective. The court asserted:

> We find it difficult to construe Article 21 to include within it the "right to die" as a part of the fundamental right guaranteed therein. "Right to life" is a natural right embodied in Article 21, but suicide is an unnatural termination or extinction of life and, therefore, incompatible and inconsistent with the concept of "right to life".[15]

The court highlighted the difference between the desirability of a law and the constitutionality of a law. Although a law may not be desirable, it could be struck down as unconstitutional only if it infringed on specific provisions of the constitution. Now, since Section 309 did not actually contravene any constitutional provision, it would stay valid. After the two-year window during which a suicide attempt was not illegal (from *Rathinam* to *Gian Kaur*), the Supreme Court restored the position that committing and abetting suicide were both punishable crimes.

The *Gian Kaur* judgement was interesting for another reason. It opened a window of opportunity to legalize euthanasia within the existing legal framework. The court held that though the

---

14 The decision in *Rathinam* was pronounced by a bench of two Supreme Court judges whereas the decision in *Gian Kaur* was pronounced by a bench of five Supreme Court judges.

15 *Gian Kaur* at para. 22.

constitutional right to life did not include the right to die, it did encompass the 'right to die with dignity'.[16] However, the right to die with dignity was not to be confused with the right to die an unnatural death, one which cut short the natural span of life. In the cases of persons who were terminally ill or in a vegetative state, the process of natural death had already commenced, and so it was possible to reason that accelerating that process would be consistent with the right to life as enshrined in the Constitution.

And then, in 2000, two remarkable 'suicide petitions' were filed in the Kerala High Court.[17] A retired octogenarian teacher felt that he had led a satisfactory life, having fulfilled all his duties and obligations, such as ensuring that his children were settled and happy. He wished to 'quit the world', but not commit suicide—a fact he acknowledged was against the law and distinguishable from his desire for a 'voluntary death'. He wanted to end his life legally by donating his organs. He wanted to highlight the difference between 'voluntary death' and suicide, based on motives. In fact, he suggested that 'voluntary death clinics' be set up in every district of Kerala to assist others who felt the same. Encouraged by this, another sixty-nine-year-old school principal made a similar plea before the high court.

The Kerala High Court rejected both petitions, affirming that suicide was suicide, regardless of the motives. As its grounds for refusing the two pleas, the court said that not only would the death of a healthy person cause a loss to society, but there was also the possibility that this 'right to die' be misused in the future.

---

16 *Gian Kaur* at para. 24.
17 *C.A. Thomas Master v. Union of India* (2000 Cr.L.J. 3729) (Kerala High Court).

How a Sprightly Nurse Ended Up As a Lifelong, Lifeless Patient

Aruna Shanbaug was a nurse at King Edward Memorial (KEM) Hospital, Mumbai (then Bombay). On the evening of 27 November 1973, Aruna, then 25, was changing her clothes in a room meant for experimental surgeries on dogs,[18] when a hospital sweeper assaulted her. Intending to rape her, he immobilized Aruna by twisting a dog chain around her neck; but when he discovered that she was menstruating, he sodomized her instead. She was found nearly twelve hours later, unconscious.

Aruna suffered acute brain damage because the oxygen supply to her brain had been blocked for a long period of time.[19] She never recovered from the attack and was relegated to the status of a helpless patient for the rest of her life. Today, forty years later, Aruna is still in a vegetative state, a lifelong patient. In 2009, journalist Pinki Virani—who had followed Aruna's life closely and also written *Aruna's Story*, a book on her life[20]—moved the Supreme Court, seeking a direction for KEM Hospital to stop feeding Aruna Shanbaug in order that she may exercise her right to die in peace and dignity.

Virani alleged that Aruna was a featherweight; her bones were brittle; her skin was like papier maché, her teeth were decayed. She had lost the ability to see and hear, as well as her complete awareness. She was fed a diet of mashed food which she could not consciously swallow. Aruna had no quality of life;

---

18 *See* Pinki Virani, *Aruna's Story: The True Account of a Rape and Its Aftermath* (New Delhi: Viking, 1998), p. 5.

19 *Aruna Shanbaug* at para. 3.

20 *See* Virani, *Aruna's Story*.

she expressed no human emotions and there was little hope of her ever recovering.

The Mumbai Municipal Corporation and the dean of KEM Hospital filed a counter-affidavit stating that Aruna accepted food normally and responded via facial expressions or intermittent sounds. The Supreme Court set up a team of three doctors to objectively report to it on Aruna's physical and mental state. The court also allowed a video recording of Aruna's condition to be screened in the courtroom. Interestingly, the court found support for conducting a screening in a courtroom from the Nuremberg trials[21] in Germany, though it is questionable whether the court should have compared the examination of Aruna's condition with Nazi atrocities during World War II! Screening the video in open court could have been avoided and the result was ironic—though the court ruled that Aruna was still 'alive' and that hers was not a case fit for euthanasia, the bench itself treated her as an inanimate object of examination. Essentially, the Supreme Court overlooked Aruna's right to privacy.

To Die or Not to Die?

The doctors' report[22] stated that Aruna seemed to be in a permanent vegetative state in many respects, but she was neither brain-dead nor comatose—she possessed some reflexes, could make symmetric facial movements, articulated some vocal sounds (though she could not respond to simple commands) and partially licked sugar smeared on her lips. The team concluded

---

21 Trials conducted after World War II for the prosecution of prominent members of the political, military and economic leadership of defeated Nazi Germany.

22 *See* Appendix II on p. 227 for the full text of the report.

that since Aruna was not in a position to take a decision, the appropriate person to do so would be the dean of KEM Hospital, since it was the hospital staff that had tended to her for thirty-seven years.

In his affidavit, the dean Dr Sanjay Oak said that Aruna should not be subjected to passive euthanasia. In fact, he asserted that India was not ready to allow the legalization of euthanasia:[23] 'I feel that the entire society has not matured enough to accept the execution of an Act of Euthanasia or Mercy Killing. I fear that this may get misused and our monitoring and deterring mechanisms may fail to prevent those unfortunate incidences.'

In its judgement, the Supreme Court endorsed the recommendation of the team of doctors that the dean was best placed to decide on the euthanasia plea as Aruna's 'next friend',[24] since the KEM Hospital staff had taken care of her for three decades when her family abandoned her. The court believed that Pinki Virani could not claim the level of attachment or bonding with Aruna that the hospital authorities could and did.[25] Also, based on reasons similar to those in the doctors' report, the court asserted that though Aruna had 'very little' brain activity, she was not brain-dead.

Since the dean had unequivocally dismissed the possibility of euthanasia for Aruna and said that she should be allowed to die a natural death, the case could have been wrapped up at that

---

23 Affidavit filed by the dean of K.E.M. Hospital in *Aruna Shanbaug* at para. 11).

24 'Next friend' refers to 'a person acting for the legal benefit of someone not legally competent to act for himself or herself'; *see* P. Ramanatha Aiyar, *Advanced Law Lexicon* (New Delhi: LexisNexis Butterworths Wadhwa Nagpur, 2009), p. 3191.

25 In the court's words: '[H]owever much her [Pinki Virani's] interest in Aruna Shanbaug may be, it cannot match the involvement of the KEM hospital staff who have been taking care of Aruna day and night for 38 years.'

stage. However, the Supreme Court chose to go beyond its call of duty, by deciding on the larger question: should euthanasia be permissible at all in India, and, if so, under what circumstances?

The court distinguished between two forms of euthanasia: active and passive. 'Active euthanasia' denotes the use of lethal substances to end a person's life, while 'passive euthanasia' entails the withholding of any medical treatment (such as life-saving antibiotics) that would ensure the survival of a patient. The difference between the two is that in case of active euthanasia the procedure that causes death would have caused the death of any person, regardless of the person's physical condition (for instance, the use of a lethal injection). This is not so in the case of passive euthanasia. In several countries, such as Ireland, passive euthanasia is permitted whereas active euthanasia is prohibited. Active euthanasia is illegal all over the United States of America while passive euthanasia is permitted in three of its states. In Mexico, active euthanasia is illegal, but passive euthanasia is permitted in Mexico City, the central state of Aguascalientes and the western state of Michoacán; the Mexican Senate has approved a law to extend the same provisions to the national level.

The Supreme Court outlined a rather tenuous distinction between an 'act' and an 'omission' to legalize passive euthanasia while reiterating the illegality of active euthanasia. It declared passive euthanasia as permissible (or, at least, not illegal), using the rationale that 'failing to save a person' could never constitute a crime. On the other hand, it confirmed that active euthanasia—because it involves a deliberate act by a third party, usually a doctor—would be tantamount to murder since death is caused by a positive 'action' rather than a mere 'omission to act'. The court offered the example of a bystander running into a burning building to rescue someone—if the bystander did not in fact try to rescue the person, he would not be guilty of committing an offence. It is questionable, though, whether a doctor administering medical treatment is comparable to a person entering a burning building to save someone. After all, a doctor does not risk his own life to administer medical aid.

The court also differentiated between voluntary and non-voluntary euthanasia. Voluntary euthanasia is when the patient is in a position to express consent while non-voluntary euthanasia is when the patient is not in such a position, being comatose for instance. Cases of non-voluntary euthanasia involve many complexities, since it is necessary that a surrogate or 'next friend' takes the decision on behalf of the patient. The Supreme Court set up a high-court-monitored mechanism to handle such cases.[26] What the court essentially did in *Aruna Shanbaug* was to follow a method it thought most appropriate and establish that method as a benchmark for all high courts to deal with cases seeking approval for passive euthanasia. The model includes appointing a team of doctors (comprising a neurologist, psychiatrist and physician) to report to the court, issue notices to the state and close relatives of the patient and so on. It would ultimately be up to the court to determine if the case were fit for permitting passive euthanasia, after considering the doctors' report and the next friend's opinion. This mechanism was to operate until Parliament passed legislation on the subject—a practice that has been employed by the Supreme Court on a few occasions, notably in *Vishaka v. State of Rajasthan*.[27]

---

26 *See* Appendix I on p. 225 for the exhaustive procedure to be followed by high courts, as outlined in the Supreme Court's judgement in *Aruna Shanbaug*.

27 AIR 1997 SC 3011.

The court also noted that if the representatives of KEM Hospital changed their decision at any stage, they would be free to move the Bombay High Court (according to the method above) with a euthanasia plea on behalf of Aruna.

It is interesting to note the sources the Supreme Court used to arrive at its decision. It relied primarily on foreign cases, even though some relevant Indian case law was available. The court discussed judgements and statutory law from regions including Canada, France, Switzerland, the Netherlands, the United Kingdom and the United States of America. It extensively cited the judgement of the House of Lords (the United Kingdom) in *Airedale NHS Trust v. Bland*,[28] in which a patient was allowed to die through the withdrawal of life-supporting treatment. The court also relied on sources such as George Bernard Shaw's play *The Doctor's Dilemma*, Robin Cook's novel *Coma* and even Google! Paragraph 103 of the judgement said that a news item the bench encountered on the internet told the story of Terry Wallis from America, who slipped into a coma after an accident in 1984, but regained consciousness twenty-four years later due to nerve regeneration in his brain. The bench also referred to a related medical case, stating 'see Terri Schiavo's case on Google'.

Thus, the window of opportunity left open by the Supreme Court in *Gian Kaur* was taken up in the *Aruna Shanbaug* case. In the latter, while the court reiterated that suicide is a criminal offence, it nevertheless permitted passive euthanasia in certain situations. In legal terms, the court held that while the 'right to life' under Article 21 includes the 'right to die with dignity', it does not include the 'right to die' per se. In other words, suicide

---

28 (1993) AC 789 HL

is illegal and punishable, but passive euthanasia is legal under certain circumstances. However, the court did recommend the deletion of Section 309 of the IPC, finding it 'anachronistic' and underscoring that a person who attempts suicide 'needs help rather than punishment'.[29]

Too 'Moral' for Courts to Decide?

The *Aruna Shanbaug* judgement has been criticized on account of the fact that the very subject of passive euthanasia hinges on a moral question. Apart from legal, there are moral arguments for and against passive euthanasia. The legislature—an elected body expected to keep its finger firmly on the pulse of public opinion—is arguably better placed to take the call.

If we were to judge the morality of the court's judgement, is the 'passive–active distinction' morally sound? The moral justification for allowing passive euthanasia against active euthanasia is not convincing. After all, depriving a patient of food (thus causing death by starvation) or antibiotics (thus causing a painful death) seems far more merciless than administering an instant and painless dose of death. The difference between the two forms of euthanasia hinges on a questionable dichotomy: 'killing' is not the same as 'allowing to die'.[30] All that it means is that in a case of passive euthanasia, the doctor can say, 'I did not kill him. His death was only expedited by an *omission to administer* medical treatment.' Well, if an act comprising active euthanasia is murder, passive euthanasia would not be very far

---

29 *Aruna Shanbaug* at para. 100.
30 Sushila Rao, 'The Moral Basis for a Right to Die', *Economic and Political Weekly*, 30 April 2011, vol. XLVI, No. 18, p. 13.

from it. The only practical difference is that active euthanasia can be abused/misused more than passive euthanasia, since even a healthy patient would die via an active euthanasia procedure. Also, unlike passive euthanasia, active euthanasia leaves no room for miracles of nature.

On the other hand, there is also significant concern over the Supreme Court's decision that Aruna Shanbaug should not be subjected to passive euthanasia. The court may have been carried away by the pleas of the dean and nurses of KEM Hospital. No one can question the dedication with which Aruna has been taken care of for close to four decades, but is it in her best interests to stay 'alive'? The 'quality of life' element and the 'best interests of the patient' test[31] should have played a much larger role in the court's judgement. Can the fact that Aruna can partially lick off sugar smeared on her lips or that she does not have bed sores justify the quality of her existence?

Another disquieting aspect of the judgement is its inherent potential to deepen the rich–poor divide. If a person from the lower middle class wishes to keep his relative (who is in a vegetative state) alive, will the state bear the monetary costs, not to mention the opportunity costs of the hospital bed dedicated to this purpose? If not, doesn't this judgement seal the fate of those who cannot afford medical care for a long period?[32]

There is also a positive aspect of the *Aruna Shanbaug* judgement. In Pinki Virani's words, 'Aruna's other gift through this same landmark judgement is that there could be a boost in organ donations, once again positively helping millions of

---

31   The Supreme Court had employed this test recently; *Suchita Srivastava v. Chandigarh Administration* (AIR 2010 SC 235).

32   Rajeev Dhavan, 'Questions about the right to die', *India Today*, 14 March 2011.

Indians. The judgement provides clarity on the definition of brain death. Healthy vital organs are wasted while arguments rage over medico-legal definition of brain death.'[33]

A Review of the Law on Euthanasia and Suicide

After *Aruna Shanbaug*, the position on euthanasia in India today is that while the law recognizes euthanasia in case of physical suffering, no amount of mental suffering would justify a claim to end a person's life. In fact, the law will penalize a suicide attempt in the latter scenario. Therefore, while relatives of a patient in a permanently vegetative state can consent to the use of a passive euthanasia procedure, a healthy adult who voluntarily attempts suicide risks being punished if his/her attempt fails. This is inconsistent. Lawmakers would do well to seriously debate the Supreme Court's recommendation to delete Section 309 of the IPC.

Doctors have documented that passive euthanasia is already practised in India today. The difference that the judgement could make is that when there is a disagreement among the patient's relatives or between the relatives and the physicians over employing a euthanasia procedure, the high court may be moved to decide on the final route to be taken.[34]

The Supreme Court's decision is added to the guidelines formulated by it that are meant to operate 'until the legislature enacts a suitable law on the issue'. There is an urgent need to

---

33 Anupama Katakam, 'Doomed to a slow death: Interview with writer and journalist Pinki Virani', *Frontline*, 26 March–8 April 2011, http://www.frontlineonnet.com/fl2807/stories/20110408280710600.htm (accessed 8 January 2013).

34 Prahlad Sethi and Nitin Sethi, 'Euthanasia and the Right to Die', *The Gangaram Journal*, vol. 1, no. 3 (2011): pp. 108–10.

comprehensively review the law on euthanasia and suicide in India—a Supreme Court judgement being used as a substitute for an enacted law should not be allowed to hold the field for too long. Many factors, including the commercialization of healthcare, the allocation/scarcity of medical resources, the development of sound mechanisms to prevent abuse of euthanasia (if permitted), and a thorough understanding of the 'active–passive distinction' should be taken into account to frame policy on the subject. One can only hope that this will not be another area of law in which the Supreme Court's decision is conveniently left by the legislature to hold the field.

One last question remains—a tough question to answer. What does one do with cases like Jan Grzebski, who regained consciousness after a nineteen-year coma caused by a brain tumour or Terry Wallis who met with a car accident and regained consciousness two decades on or Dan Cassil, who was revived from a deep coma on hearing his favourite TV show *Seinfeld*?

APPENDIX I

The following, excerpted from the Supreme Court ruling in *Aruna Shanbaug*,[35] sets out the procedure to be adopted by high courts when an application for 'non-voluntary euthanasia' is filed.

❖ On the filing of an application for 'non-voluntary euthanasia', the Chief Justice of the High Court should forthwith constitute a bench of at least two judges who should decide to grant approval or not. Before doing so, the bench should seek the opinion of a committee of three reputed doctors to be nominated by the bench after consulting such medical authorities/practitioners as it may deem fit. Preferably, one of the three doctors should be a neurologist, one a psychiatrist, and one a physician. For this purpose, a panel of doctors in every city may be prepared by the high court in consultation with the state government/Union Territory, and their fees for this purpose may be fixed beforehand.

❖ The committee of three doctors nominated by the bench should carefully examine the patient and also consult the record of the patient as well as take the views of the hospital staff and submit its report to the bench.

❖ Simultaneously, with the appointment of the committee of doctors, the bench shall also issue notice to the State and close relatives (for example, the parents, spouse, brother(s)/ sister(s)) of the patient, and in their absence his/her next friend, and supply a copy of the report of the doctor's committee to them as soon as it is available. After hearing

35 Paragraphs 138–42.

them, the bench should give its verdict. The above procedure should be followed all over India until the Parliament makes legislation on this subject.

❖ The high court should give its decision at the earliest, since a delay in the matter may result in causing great mental agony to the relatives and persons close to the patient.

❖ The high court should give its decision assigning specific reasons in accordance with the principle of 'best interest of the patient' laid down by the House of Lords in Airedale's case. The views of the near relatives and committee of doctors should be given due weight by the high court before pronouncing a final verdict which shall not be summary in nature.

APPENDIX II

The following report, directly excerpted from the Supreme Court ruling in *Aruna Shanbaug*, was submitted by the team of doctors to the Supreme Court, examining the physical and mental condition of Ms Aruna Shanbaug.

Report of examination of Ms Aruna Ramachandra Shanbaug jointly prepared and signed by:
1. Dr J.V. Divatia (Professor and Head, Department of Anaesthesia, Critical Care and Pain, at Tata Memorial Hospital, Mumbai)
2. Dr Roop Gursahani (Consultant Neurologist at P.D. Hinduja Hospital, Mumbai)
3. Dr Nilesh Shah (Professor and Head, Department of Psychiatry at Lokmanya Tilak Municipal Corporation Medical College and General Hospital)

I. Background

As per the request of Hon. Justice Katju and Hon. Justice Mishra of the Supreme Court of India, Ms Aruna Ramachandra Shanbaug, a 60-year-old female patient was examined on the morning of 28 January 2011, and 3 February 2011, in the side-room of ward-4, of the K.E.M. Hospital by a team of three doctors viz., Dr J.V. Divatia (Professor and Head, Department of Anaesthesia, Critical Care and Pain at Tata Memorial Hospital, Mumbai), Dr Roop Gursahani (Consultant Neurologist at P.D. Hinduja Hospital, Mumbai) and Dr Nilesh Shah (Professor and Head, Department of Psychiatry at Lokmanya Tilak

Municipal Corporation Medical College and General Hospital, Mumbai).

This committee was set up because the court found some variance between the allegations in the writ petition filed by Ms Pinki Virani on behalf of Aruna Ramachandra Shanbaug and the counter-affidavit of Dr Pazare. This team of three doctors was appointed to examine Aruna Ramachandra Shanbaug thoroughly and give a report to the Court about her physical and mental condition.

It was felt by the team of doctors appointed by the Supreme Court that longitudinal case history and observations of the last thirty-seven years along with findings of the examination will give a better, clear and comprehensive picture of the patient's condition.

This report is based on:

1. The longitudinal case history and observations obtained from the dean and the medical and nursing staff of K.E.M. Hospital;
2. Case records (including nursing records) since January 2010;
3. Findings of the physical, neurological and mental status examinations performed by the panel; and
4. Investigations performed during the course of this assessment (blood tests, CT head, electroencephalogram).

II. Medical History

The medical history of Ms Aruna Ramachandra Shanbaug was obtained from the dean, the principal of the School of Nursing, and the medical and nursing staff of ward-4 who have been looking after her.

It was learnt from the persons mentioned above that:

1. Ms Aruna Ramachandra Shanbaug was admitted in the hospital after she was assaulted and strangulated by a sweeper of the hospital on 27 November 1973.

2. Though she survived, she never fully recovered from the trauma and brain damage resulting from the assault and strangulation.

3. Since the last many years she has been in the same bed in the side-room of ward-4.

4. The hospital staff has provided her with excellent nursing care since then, which included feeding her by mouth, bathing her and taking care of her toilet needs. The care was of such an exceptional nature that she has not developed a single bed sore or fracture in spite of her bedridden state since 1973.

5. According to the history related by them, though she is not too aware of herself and her surroundings, she somehow recognizes the presence of people around her and expresses her like or dislike by making certain types of vocal sounds and waving her hands in certain manners. She appears to be happy and smiles when she receives her favourite food items like fish and chicken soup. She accepts food which she likes, but may spit out food she doesn't like. She was able to take oral feeds till 16 September 2010, which is when she developed a febrile illness, probably malaria. After that, her oral intake reduced and a feeding tube (Ryle's tube) was passed into her stomach via her nose. Since then she receives her major feeds from the Ryle's tube, and is only occasionally able to accept oral liquids. Malaria has taken a toll on her physical condition, but she is gradually recuperating from it.

6. Occasionally, when there are many people in the room she makes vocal sounds indicating distress. She calms down when people move out of her room. She also seems to enjoy the devotional songs and music which is played in her room and it has a calming effect on her.

7. In an annual ritual, each and every batch of nursing students is introduced to Ms Aruna Ramachandra Shanbaug, and is told that 'She was one of us'; 'She was a very nice and efficient staff nurse, but due to the mishap she is in this bedridden state'.

8. The entire nursing staff and other staff members have a very compassionate attitude towards Ms Aruna Ramachandra Shanbaug and they all, very happily and willingly, take care of her. They all are very proud of their achievement of taking such good care of their bedridden colleague and feel very strongly that they want to continue to take care of her in the same manner till she succumbs naturally. They do not feel that Ms Aruna Ramachandra Shanbaug is living a painful and miserable life.

III. Examination

IIIa. Physical Examination

She was conscious, but unable to cooperate and appeared to be unaware of her surroundings. Her body was lean and thin. She appeared neat and clean and lay curled up in the bed with movements of the left hand and made sounds, especially when many people were present in the room.

She was afebrile, and her pulse rate was 80/min, regular and good volume. Her blood pressure recorded on the nursing charts was normal. Respiratory rate was 15/min, regular, with no signs of respiratory distress or breathlessness. There was no pallor, cyanosis, clubbing or icterus. She was edentulous (lacking teeth). Skin appeared to be generally in good condition; there were no bed sores, bruises or evidence of old healed bed sores. There were no skin signs suggestive of nutritional deficiency or dehydration. Her wrists had developed severe contractures, and were fixed in acute flexion. Both knees had also developed contractures (right more than left). A nasogastric feeding tube (Ryle's tube) was in situ. She was wearing diapers.

Abdominal, respiratory and cardiovascular examination was unremarkable.

IIIb. Neurological Examination

When examined she was conscious with eyes open, wakefulness but without any apparent awareness (*see* Table 1 for detailed assessment of awareness). From the above examination, she has evidence of intact auditory, visual, somatic and motor primary neural pathways. However, no definitive evidence for awareness of auditory, visual, somatic and motor stimuli was observed during our examinations.

There was no coherent response to verbal commands or to calling her name. She did not turn her head to the direction of sounds or voices. When roused she made non-specific unintelligible sounds ('uhhh, ahhh') loudly and continuously, but was generally silent when undisturbed.

Menace reflex (blinking in response to hand movements in front of eyes) was present in both eyes and hemifields, but brisker and more consistent on the left. Pupillary reaction was normal bilaterally. Fundi could not be seen since she closed her eyes tightly when this was attempted. At rest she seemed to maintain preferential gaze to the left, but otherwise gaze was random and undirected (roving) though largely conjugate. Facial movements were symmetric. Gag reflex (movement of the palate in response to insertion of a tongue depressor in the throat) was present and she does not pool saliva. She could swallow both teaspoonfuls of water as well as a small quantity of mashed banana. She licked, though not very completely, sugar smeared on her lips, suggesting some tongue control.

She had flexion contractures of all limbs and seemed to be incapable of turning in bed spontaneously. There was what appeared to be minimal voluntary movement with the left upper limb (touching her wrist to the eye for instance, perhaps as an attempt to rub it). When examined/disturbed, she seemed to curl up even further in her flexed foetal position. Sensory examination was not possible, but she did seem to find passive movement painful in all four limbs and moaned continuously during the examination. Deep tendon reflexes were difficult to elicit elsewhere, but were present at the ankles. Plantars were withdrawal/extensor.

Thus, neurologically, she appears to be in a state of intact consciousness without awareness of self/environment. No cognitive or communication abilities could be discerned. Visual function, if present, is severely limited. Motor function is grossly impaired with quadriparesis.

IIIc. Mental Status Examination

1. Consciousness, General Appearance, Attitude and
   Behaviour: Ms Aruna Ramachandra Shanbaug was resting
   quietly in her bed, apparently listening to devotional music,
   when we entered the room. Though her body build is lean,
   she appeared to be well nourished and there were no signs
   of malnourishment. She appeared neat and clean. She has
   developed contractures at both the wrist joints and knee
   joints and so lay curled up in the bed with minimum,
   restricted physical movements.

   She was conscious, but appeared to be unaware of herself
   and her surroundings. As soon as she realized the presence of
   some people in her room, she started making repetitive vocal
   sounds and moving her hands. This behaviour subsided as we
   left the room. She did not have any involuntary movements.
   She did not demonstrate any catatonic, hostile or violent
   behaviour.

   Her eyes were wide open and from her behaviour it
   appeared that she could see and hear us, as when one loudly
   called her name, she stopped making vocal sounds and hand
   movements for a while. She was unable to maintain sustained
   eye-to eye contact, but when the hand was suddenly taken
   near her eyes, she was able to blink well.

   When an attempt was made to feed her by mouth,
   she accepted a spoonful of water, some sugar and mashed
   banana. She also licked the sugar and banana paste sticking
   on her upper lips and swallowed it. Thus, at times, she could
   cooperate when fed.

2. Mood and effect: It was difficult to assess her mood as she was
    unable to communicate or express her feelings. She appeared
    to calm down when she was touched or caressed gently. She
    did not cry or laugh or express any other emotions verbally
    or non-verbally during the examination period. When not
    disturbed and observed quietly from a distance, she did
    not appear to be in severe pain or misery. Only when many
    people enter her room, she appears to get a bit disturbed
    about it.
3. Speech and thoughts: She could make repeated vocal sounds
    but she could not utter or repeat any comprehensible words
    or follow and respond to any of the simple commands (such
    as 'show me your tongue'). The only way she expressed
    herself was by making some sounds. She appeared to have
    minimal language comprehension or expression.
4. Perception: She did not appear to be having any perceptual
    abnormality like hallucinations or illusions from her
    behaviour.
5. Orientation, memory and intellectual capacity: Formal
    assessment of orientation in time, place and person, memory
    of immediate, recent and remote events and her intellectual
    capacity could not be carried out.
6. Insight: As she does not appear to be fully aware of herself
    and her surroundings, she is unlikely to have any insight
    into her illness.

IV. Reports of Investigations

IVa. CT Scan Head (Plain)

This is contaminated by movement artefacts. It shows generalized prominence of supratentorial sulci and ventricles suggestive of generalized cerebral atrophy. Brainstem and cerebellum seem normal. Ischaemic foci are seen in left centrum semiovale and right external capsule. In addition a small left parieto-occipital cortical lesion is also seen and is probably ischaemic.

IVb. EEG

The dominant feature is a moderately rhythmic alpha frequency at 8-10 Hz and 20-70 microvolts which is widely distributed and is equally prominent both anteriorly and posteriorly. It is not responsive to eye-opening as seen on the video. Beta at 18-25 Hz is also seen diffusely but more prominently anteriorly. No focal or paroxysmal abnormalities were noted.

IVc. Blood

Reports of the haemoglobin, white cell count, liver function tests, renal function tests, electrolytes, thyroid function, Vitamin B12 and 1, 25 dihydroxy Vit D3 levels are unremarkable.

V. Diagnostic Impression

1. From the longitudinal case history and examination, it appears that Ms Aruna Ramachandra Shanbaug has

developed non-progressive, but irreversible brain damage secondary to hypoxic-ischaemic brain injury consistent with the known effects of strangulation. Most authorities consider a period exceeding four weeks in this condition, especially when due to hypoxic-ischaemic injury as confirming irreversibility. In Ms Aruna's case, this period has been as long as thirty-seven years, making her perhaps the longest survivor in this situation.

2. She meets most of the criteria for being in a permanent vegetative state (PVS). PVS is defined as a clinical condition of unawareness (Table 1) of self and environment in which the patient breathes spontaneously, has a stable circulation and shows cycles of eye closure and opening which may simulate sleep and waking (Table 2). While she has evidence of intact auditory, visual, somatic and motor primary neural pathways, no definitive evidence for awareness of auditory, visual, somatic and motor stimuli was observed during our examinations.

VI. Prognosis

Her dementia has not progressed and has remained stable for last many years and it is likely to remain same over next many years. At present there is no treatment available for the brain damage she has sustained.

VII. Appendix

VII(a) Table 1. Clinical Assessment to Establish Unawareness[36]

Domain Observed	Stimulus	Response
Auditory Awareness	Sudden loud noise (clap)	Startle present, ceases other movements
	Meaningful noise (rattled steel tumbler and spoon, film songs of 1970s)	Non-specific head and body movements
	Spoken commands ('close your eyes', 'lift left hand' in English, Marathi and Konkani)	Unable to obey commands
		No specific or reproducible response
Visual Awareness	Bright light to eyes	Pupillary responses present
	Large moving object in front of eyes (bright red torch rattle)	Tracking movements: present, but inconsistent and poorly reproducible
	Visual threat (fingers suddenly moved toward eyes)	Blinks, but more consistent on left than right
	Written command (English, Marathi: 'close your eyes')	No response
Somatic Awareness	Painful stimuli to limbs (light prick with sharp end of tendon hammer)	Withdrawal, maximal in left upper limb
	Painful stimuli to face	Distress, but no coordinated response to remove stimulus
	Routine sensory stimuli during care (changing position in bed and feeding)	Generalized non-specific response present, but no coordinated attempt to assist in process
Motor Output	Spontaneous	Non-specific undirected activities. Goal directed: lifting left hand to left side of face, apparently to rub her left eye
	Responsive	Non-specific undirected without any goal-directed activities

---

36 D.T. Wade and C. Johnston, 'The Permanent Vegetative State: Practical Guidance on Diagnosis and Management', *British Medical Journal*, vol. 319 (1999): pp. 841–44.

Conclusion: From the above examination, she has evidence of intact auditory, visual, somatic and motor primary neural pathways. However, no definitive evidence for awareness of auditory, visual, somatic and motor stimuli was observed during our examinations.

VII(b) Table 2. Application of Criteria for Vegetative State[37]

Criteria	Examination findings: whether she meets criteria (Yes/No/Probably)
Unaware of self and environment	Yes, unaware
No interaction with others	Yes, no interaction
No sustained, reproducible or purposeful voluntary behavioural response to visual, auditory, tactile or noxious stimuli	Yes, no sustained, reproducible or purposeful behavioural response, but: (1) Resisted examination of fundus (2) Licked sugar off lips
No language comprehension	Yes, no comprehension expression
No blink to visual threat	Blinks, but more consistent on left than right
Present sleep–wake cycles	Yes (according to nurses)
Preserved autonomic and hypothalamic function	Yes
Preserved cranial nerve reflexes	Yes
Bowel and bladder incontinence	Yes

37 J.L. Bernat, 'Current Controversies in States of Chronic Unconsciousness', *Neurology Clinical Practice*, vol. 75 (suppl. 1) (2010): pp. S33–S38.